AF618234

gefördert durch supported by

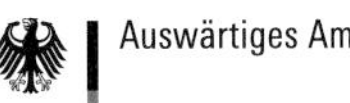

herausgeber editor
harald theiss

bauhaus

GESEHEN VON SEEN BY STEFAN BERG

texte texts
harald theiss
wiebke loeper

DISTANZ

4

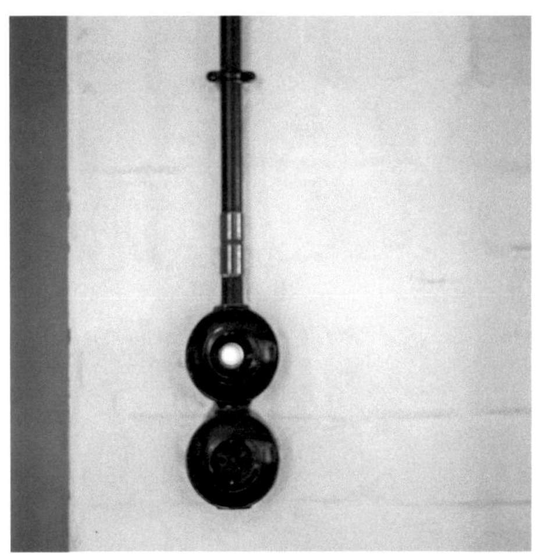

bauhaus gesehen von stefan berg

EIN TEXT VON HARALD THEISS

das bauhaus gilt weltweit als heimstätte der avantgarde der klassischen moderne und ist stilprägend für nachfolgende generationen geblieben. mit rationaler architektur und schlichtem design avancierte es zum mythos. es ist nicht nur das weiße kubische haus mit dem flachdach, dem stahlrohrsessel oder der lampe aus opalglas. das bauhaus war vor allem ein denkmodell. es hat eine neue geistige haltung sichtbar gemacht: das anstreben von „gemeinsamkeit im geistigen", wie gropius es nannte, ein bauhaus der experimente und der visionen. es sind die ideen, gedanken und abstraktionen, die sich zu einem gesamtbild zusammenfügen und bis heute eine internationale wirkung haben. ein kreativer raum wird sichtbar und begehbar. stefan berg gelingt es, am beispiel des bauhausgebäudes dessau über das medium der fotografie dieses kulturelle erbe der moderne und den damaligen neuen geist auf eine neue art zu betrachten. sein fotografischer beitrag ermöglicht eine zeitgenössische perspektive auf die ästhetik des konstruktivismus, des funktionalismus und der neuen sachlichkeit, deren abstrakte wahrnehmung bis heute einfluss auf nachfolgende architekten- und designergenerationen ausgeübt hat. in einem gespräch über seine motivation antwortete der ausgebildete fotograf, er wolle die idee bauhaus ohne einen historischen, dokumentarischen oder architekturtheoretischen begleittext anderen erfahrbar und sichtbar machen. das medium der fotografie und dessen experimentelle möglichkeiten erlaubten ihm zu zeigen, wie sich diese idee im gebäude artikuliert und spürbar wird. berg gelingt ein ästhetisches erlebnis und gleichzeitig eine zeitgenössische betrachtung. die fotografierte architektur erzeugt eine vielfalt von stimmungsbildern, ähnlich wie beim lesen eines buches, bei dem nicht das sehen der einzelnen buchstaben in uns die gefühle hervorruft, sondern die geschichte, die erzählt wird. das bauhausgebäude dessau fordert ihn zum denken im fotografieren auf. das erinnert an die genau überlegten bildkompositionen von sigfried giedion, der an seinen freund walter gropius schrieb: „gewöhnlich fotografiere ich ja selbst, (...) vor allem um es so zu haben, wie man es braucht, um möglichst wenig worte daran zu hängen." *

stefan bergs fotografisches interesse ist es vor allem, das gebäude grafisch und gestalterisch erfahrbar zu machen, indem er nach gestaltungselementen und gleichzeitig nach inhalten sucht, die aufeinander bezug nehmen und miteinander korrespondieren. seine bilder zeigen, wie die äußerlich gestaltete asymmetrie der kubisch geformten baukörper im inneren symmetrisch wird. wie durch das durchdringen und das spiel von licht der außenraum mit dem innenraum verschmilzt und wie sichtbarer funktionalismus zu rauminstallationen werden kann. mit seinen bebilderten kapiteleinleitungen ist das buch ein fotografischer parcours zum, im und um das bauhausgebäude dessau. dabei spielt für das verständnis die zusammenstellung und der dialog der bilder eine wesentliche rolle. über eine zeitgenössische bildsprache und losgelöst vom allgemein bekannten kulturhistorischen und architektonischen diskurs wird das modell ‚bauhaus denken' in der gegenwart sichtbar.
es ermöglicht ein neues sehen und reflektiert einen gestaltungswillen, der über einen rein ästhetischen anspruch hinausreicht. er war gleichzeitig ein ausdruck von modernisierung. das bauhaus setzte vor 100 jahren weltweit neue maßstäbe für architektur und kunst und wurde gleichzeitig zum protagonisten für einen gesellschaftlichen wandel. es prägte damit nicht nur einen gestaltungsbegriff, sondern auch ein lebensmodell. diese idee vom neugestalten ist heute wieder aktuell, weil sich unsere gesellschaft erneut im umbruch befindet. es muss nicht alles bauhaus sein, aber ohne diese denkschule und vorstellung vom leben wäre heute vieles nichts.

* werner oechslin und gregor harbusch (hrsg.): sigfried giedion und die fotografie, gta zürich, 2010

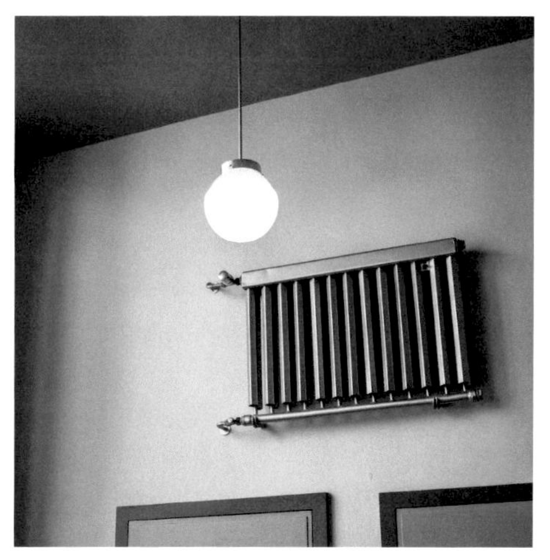

bauhaus seen by stefan berg

A TEXT BY HARALD THEISS

the bauhaus is regarded worldwide as the home of classic modernism's avant-garde and has remained formative for subsequent generations of designers and artists. with rational architecture and sober design, it became a myth. it is not only the flat-roofed, white cubic building, tubular steel armchair or lamp made of opal glass. the bauhaus was, above all, a school of thought. it made a new mental attitude visible: the aspiration of 'commonality in the spiritual', as gropius called it, a bauhaus of experiments and visions. it is the ideas, thoughts and abstractions that come together to form an overall picture and have an international effect to this day. a creative space is made visible and navigable. stefan berg succeeds in regarding this modern cultural heritage and once new spirit through the medium of photography, taking the bauhaus building in dessau as an example. his photographic contribution enables a contemporary perspective on the aesthetics of constructivism, functionalism and 'die neue sachlichkeit' (the new objectivity), whose abstract perception has exercised influence on ensuing generations of architects and designers. in a conversation about his motivation, the photographer answered that he wants to make the idea of the bauhaus visible and able to be experienced without an accompanying historical, documentary or architecture-theoretical text. the medium of photography and its experimental possibilities allows him to show how this idea is articulated and made traceable in the building itself. berg successfully creates an aesthetic experience and, simultaneously, a contemporary observation. the photographed architecture evokes a wide variety of moods, similar to reading a book, where it is not the individual letters that arouse emotions in us, but the story that is told with and through them. the bauhaus building in dessau challenges him to think in the form of photography. this is reminiscent of the carefully considered pictorial compositions of sigfried giedion, who wrote to his friend walter gropius: "i photograph habitually (...) above all to have it precisely as one needs it, in order to hang as few words as necessary on it." *

stefan berg's main interest in photography is to make the building graphically and artistically palpable, by searching for design elements and at the same time for subjects that refer to each other and correspond with each other. his photographs show how the designed asymmetry on the outside of the cube-shaped building becomes symmetric on the inside; how through the interpenetration and play of light the space outside fuses with the inside; and how conspicuous functionalism can become spatial installations.

with its illustrated chapter introductions, the book is a photographic obstacle course to, in and around the bauhaus building in dessau. the combination and dialog of the images plays an essential role in this understanding. through a contemporary visual language detached from the commonly known culture-historical and architectural discourse, the model of 'bauhaus thinking' becomes visible in the present. it enables a new way of seeing and reflects a creative will that goes beyond a purely aesthetic claim. it was, at the same time, an expression of modernization. 100 years ago, the bauhaus set new standards for architecture and art worldwide and simultaneously became a protagonist for social change. it not only minted a conception of design, but also a model of life. this idea of reinvention is relevant again today while our society yet again undergoes radical change. Not everything has to be bauhaus, but without this school of thought and imagination of life many things would be nothing.

* werner oechslin and gregor harbusch (eds.): sigfried giedion und die fotografie, gta zürich, 2010

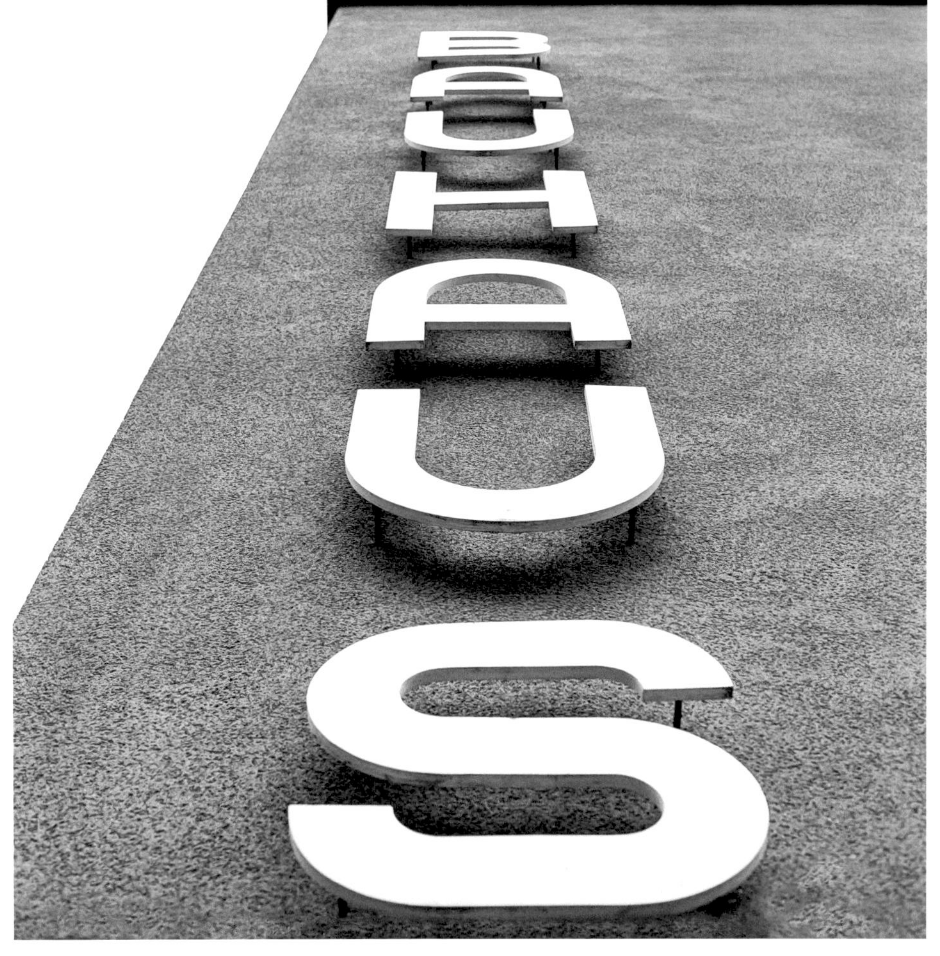
BAUHAUS

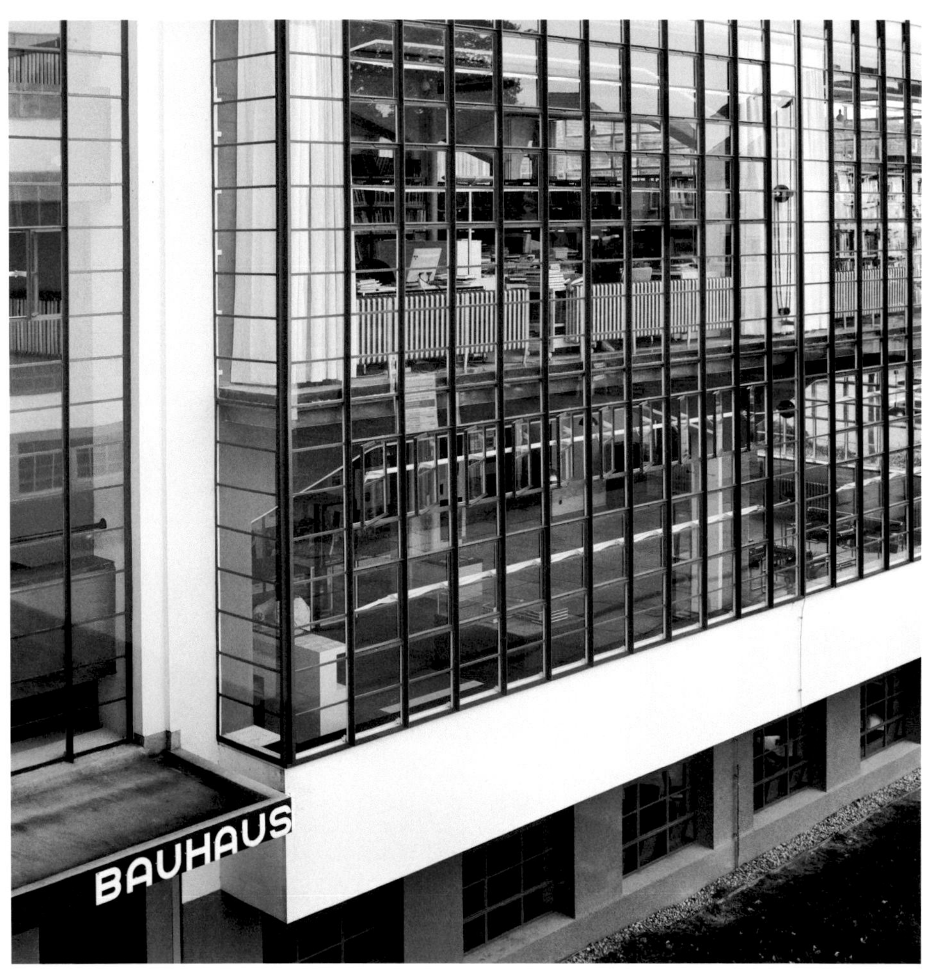
BAUHAUS

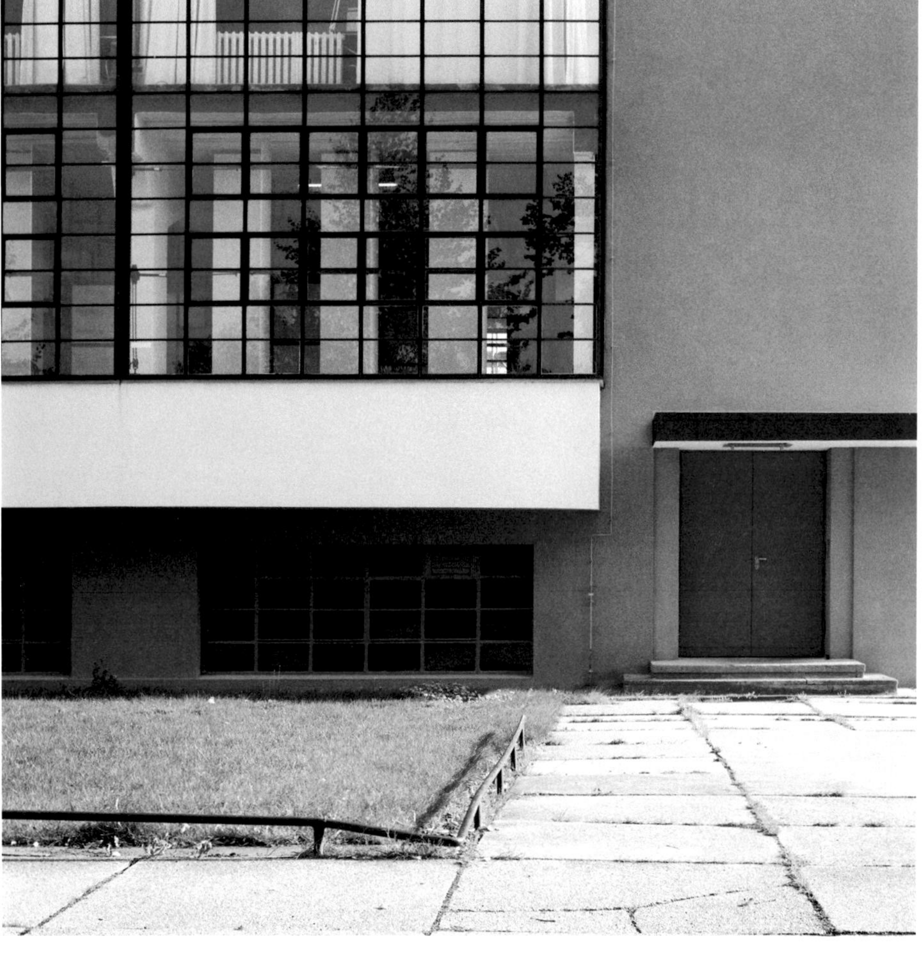

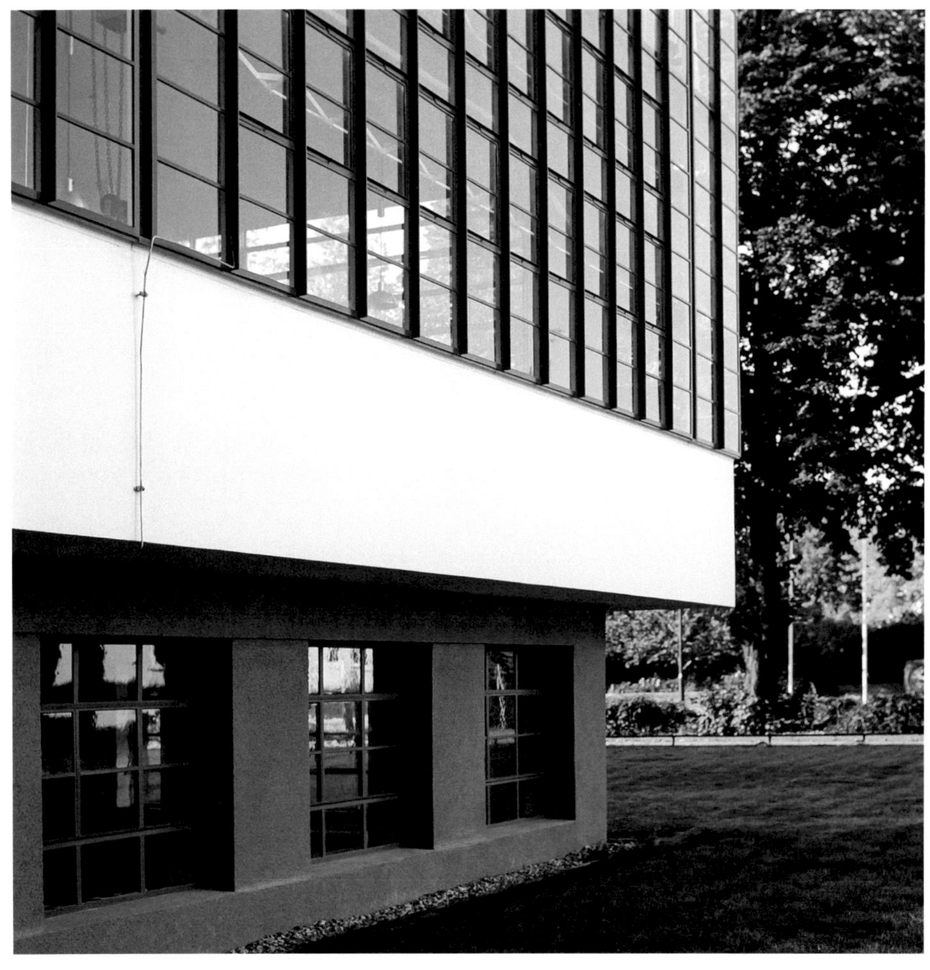

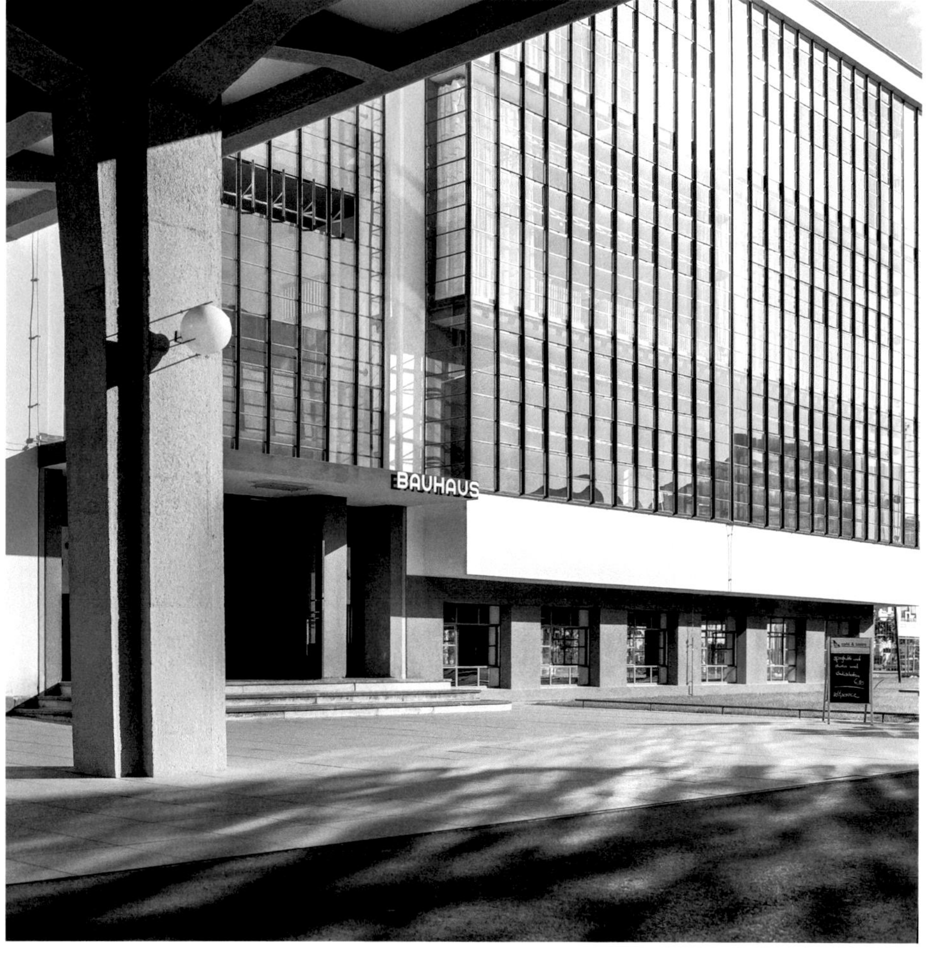
BAUHAUS

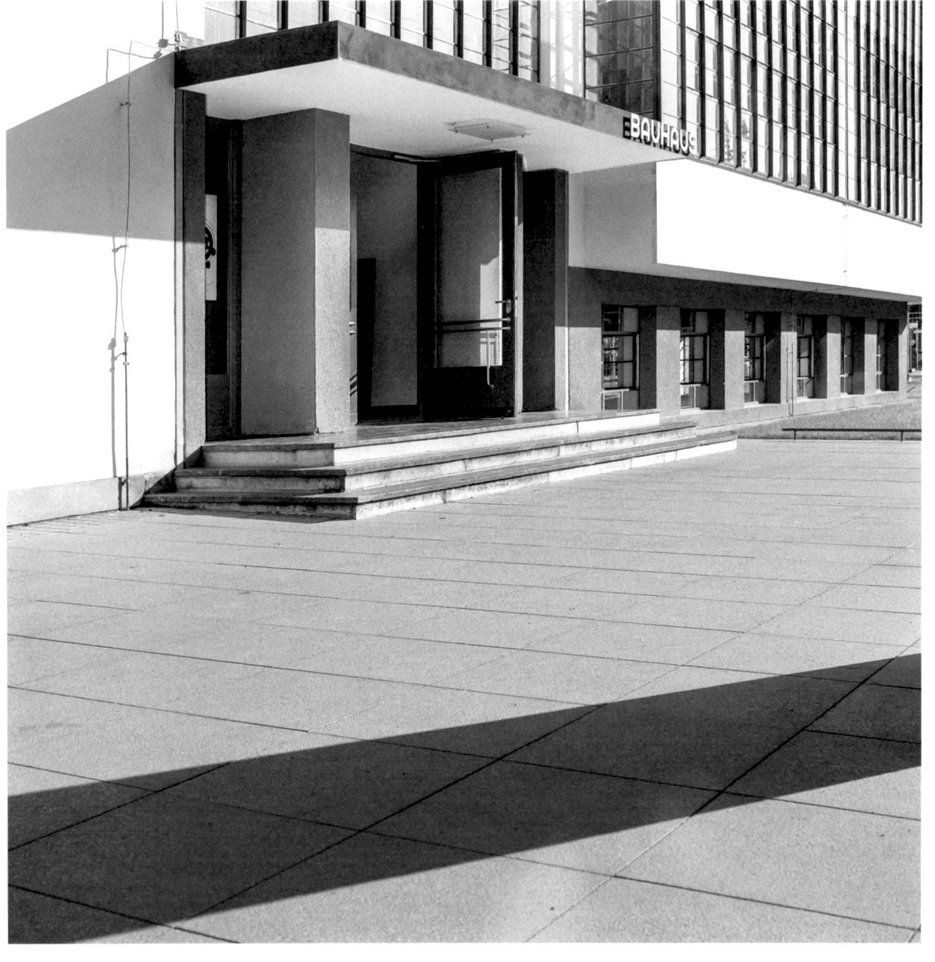
BAUHAUS

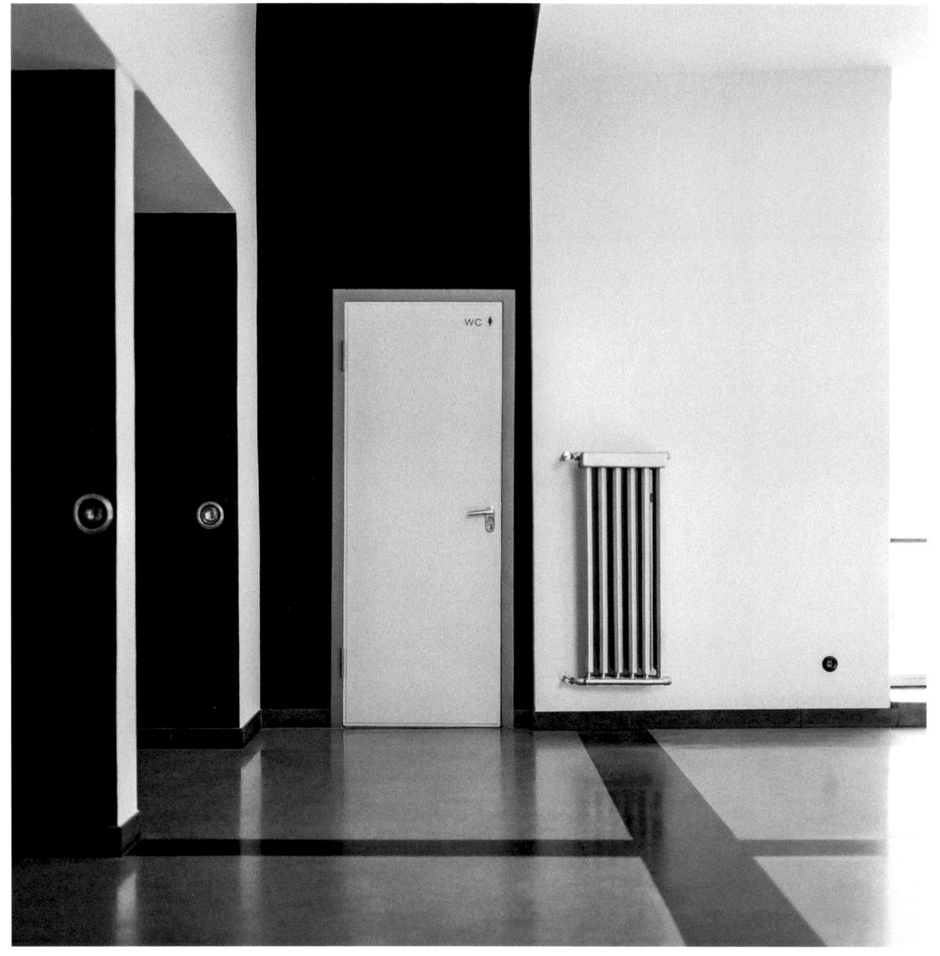
WC

20

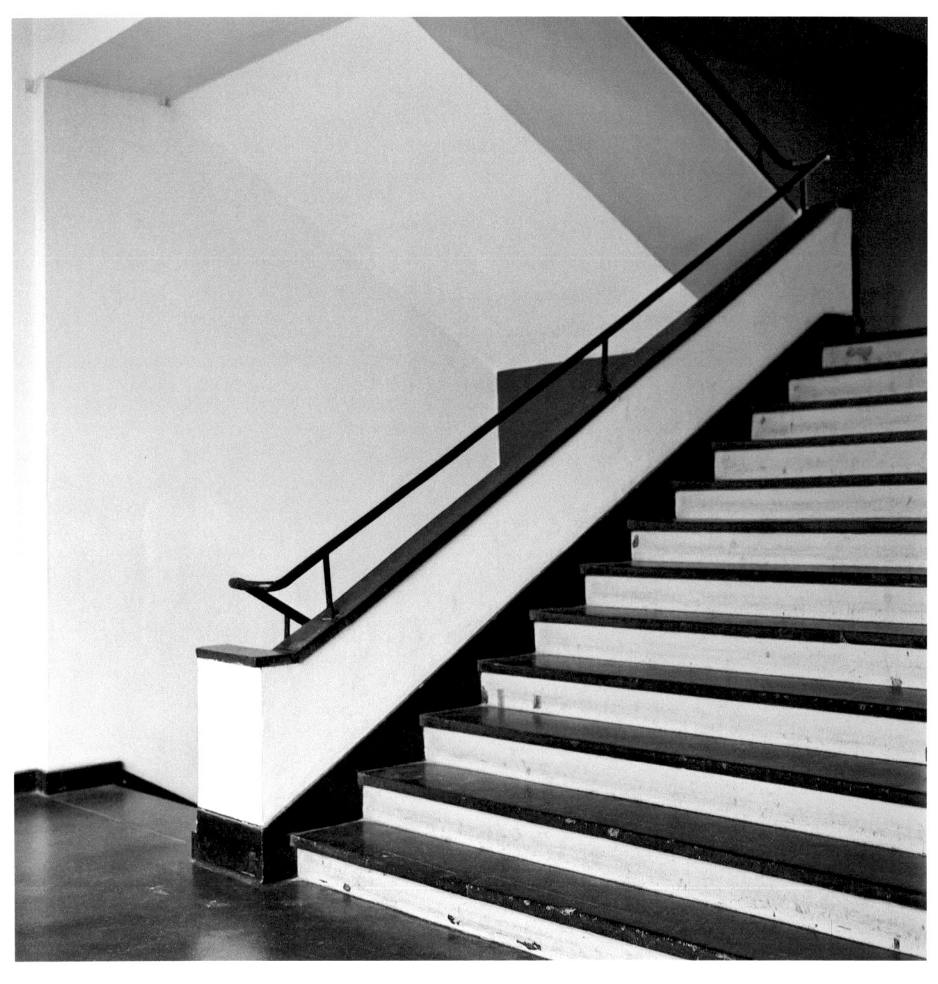

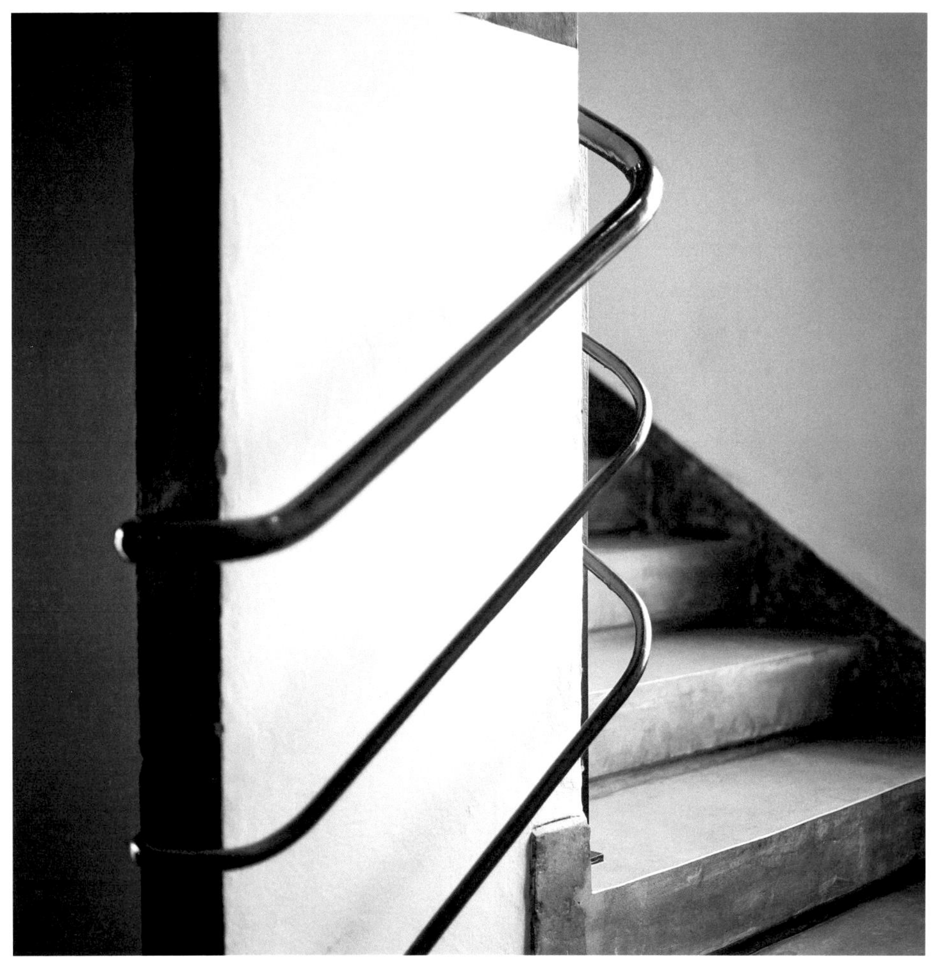

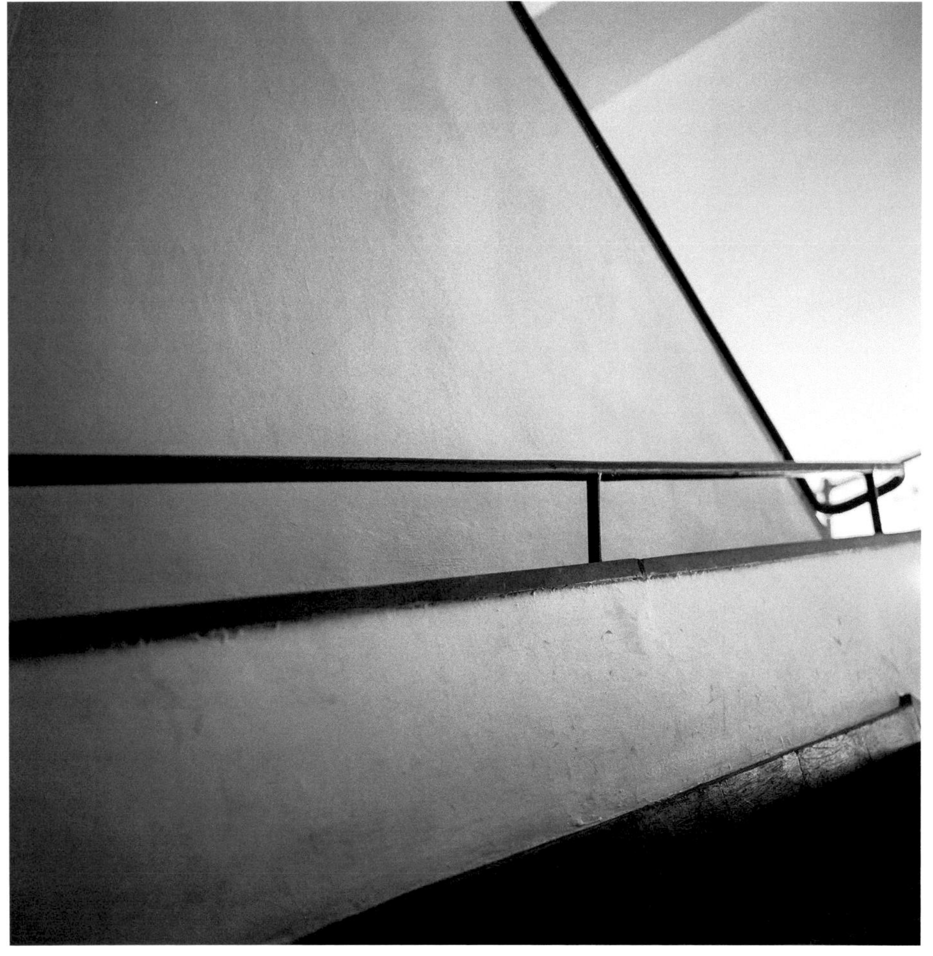

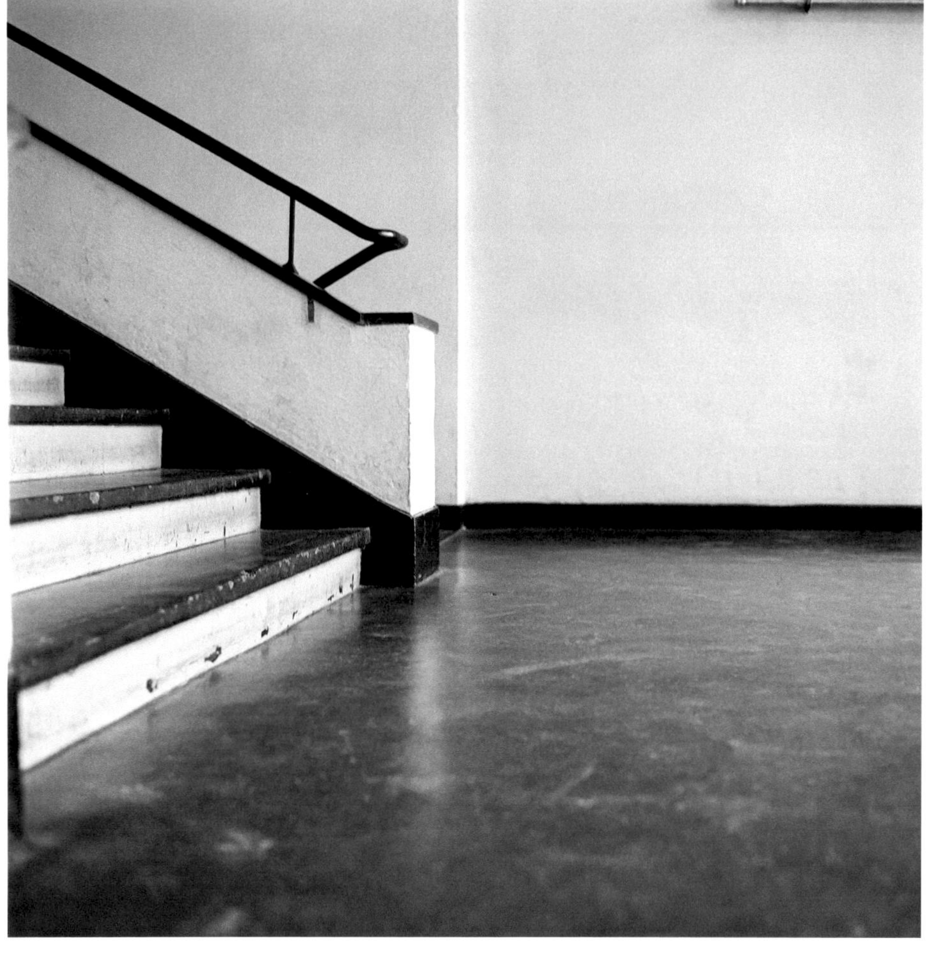

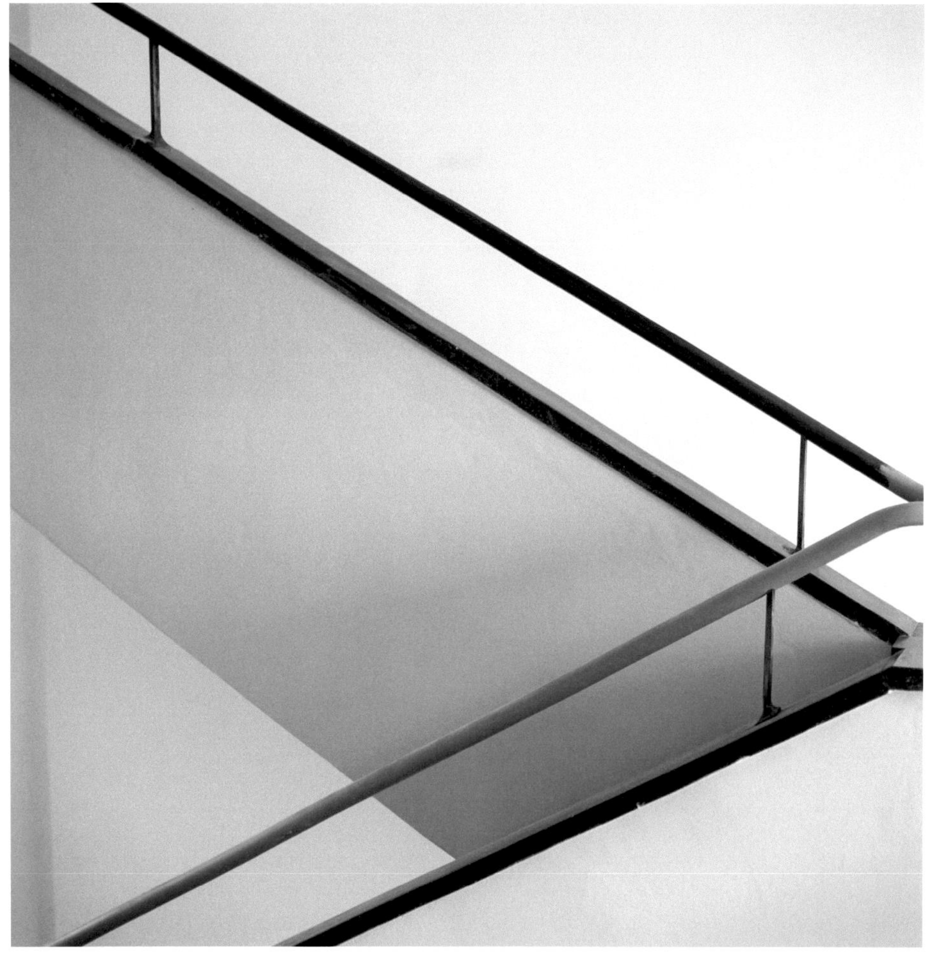

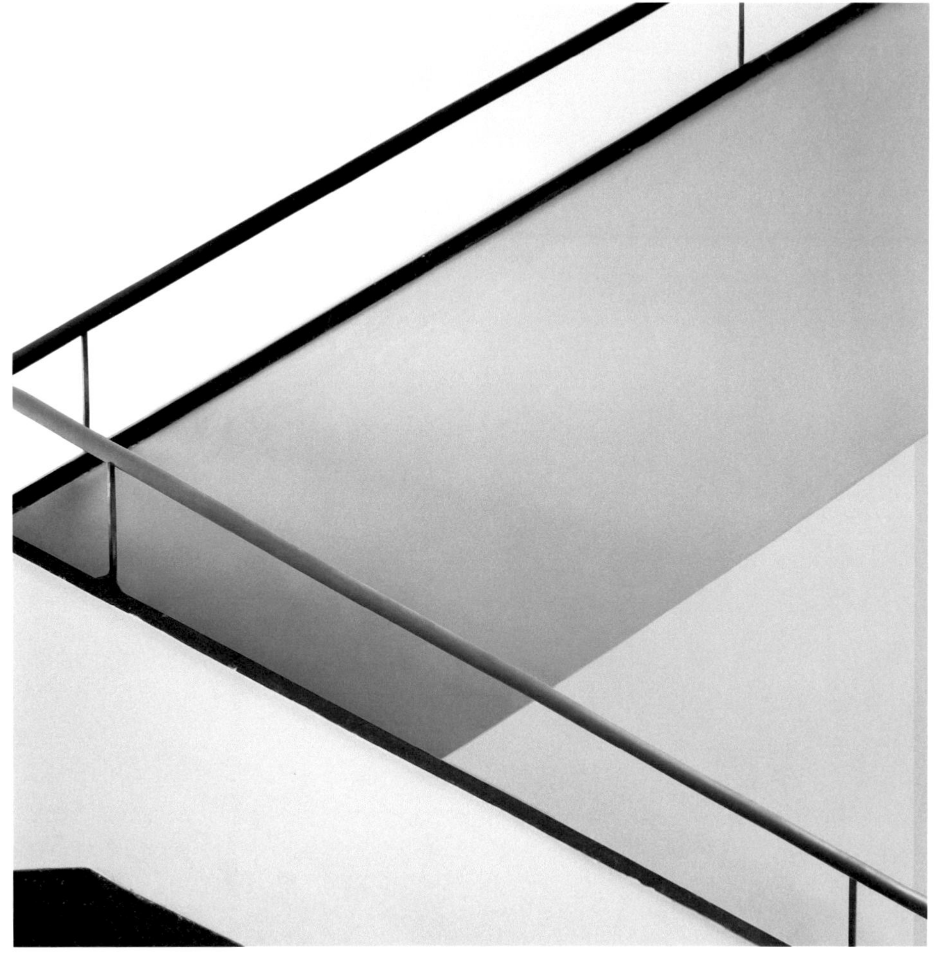

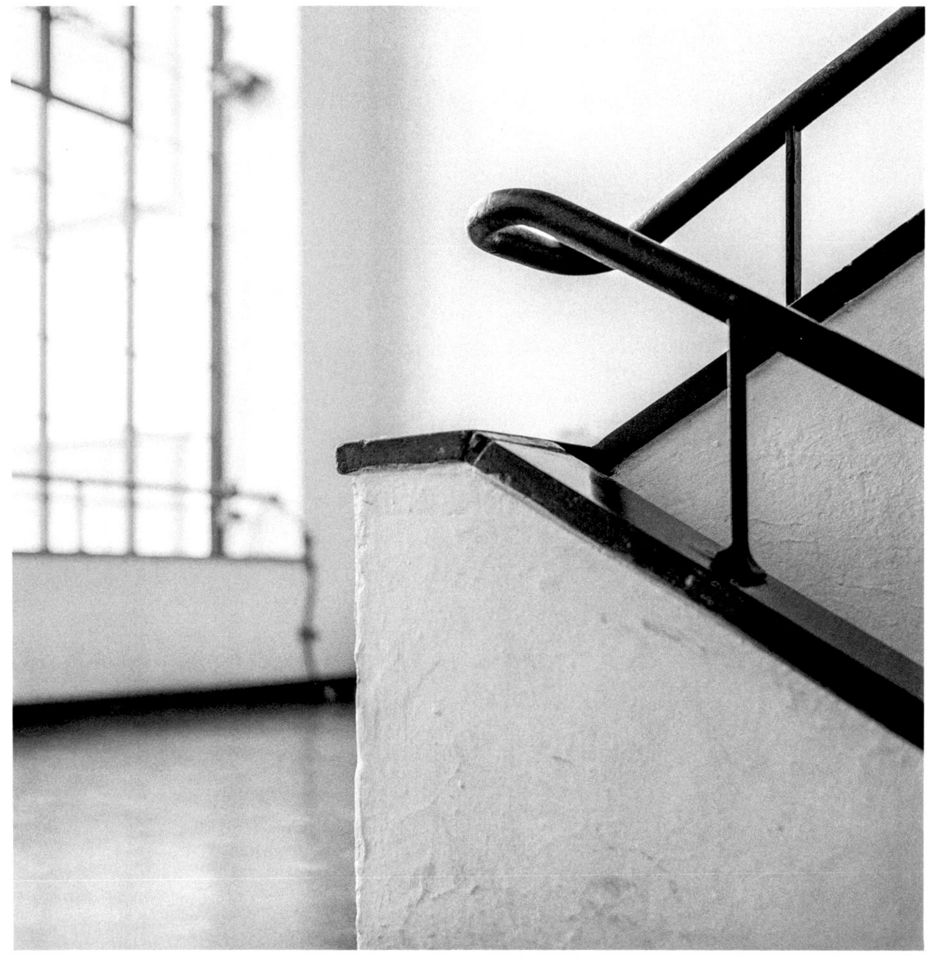

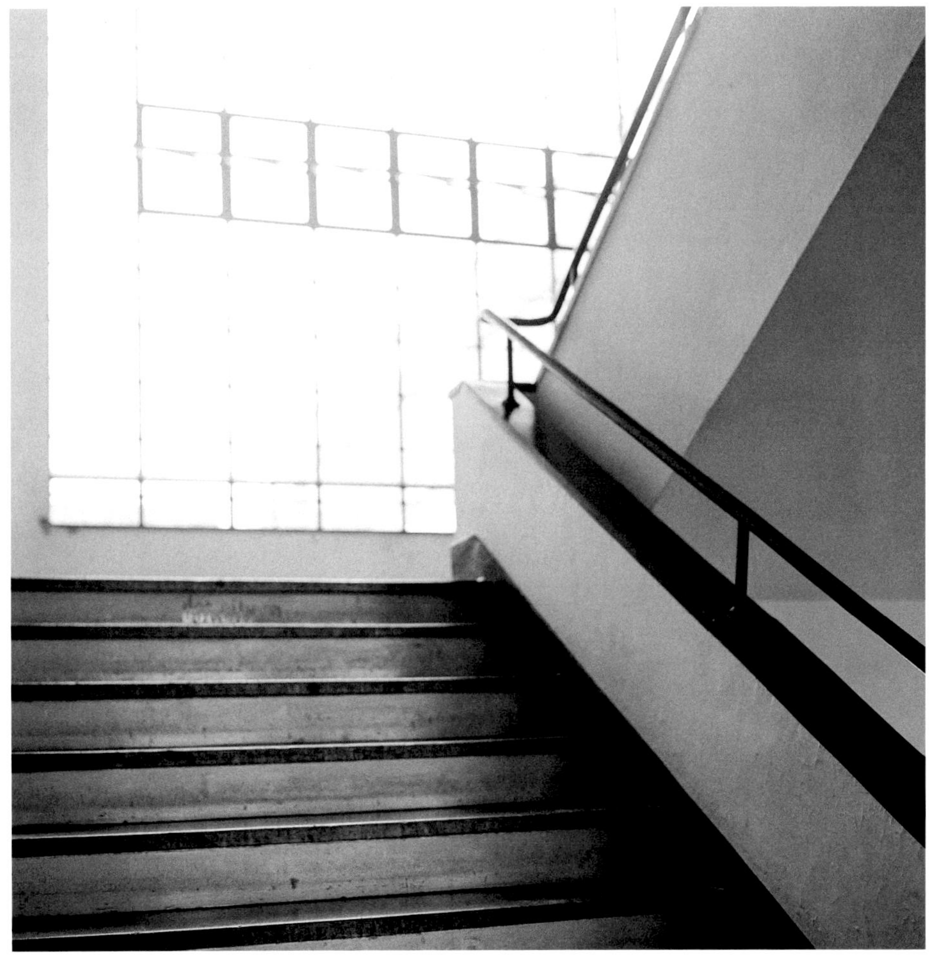

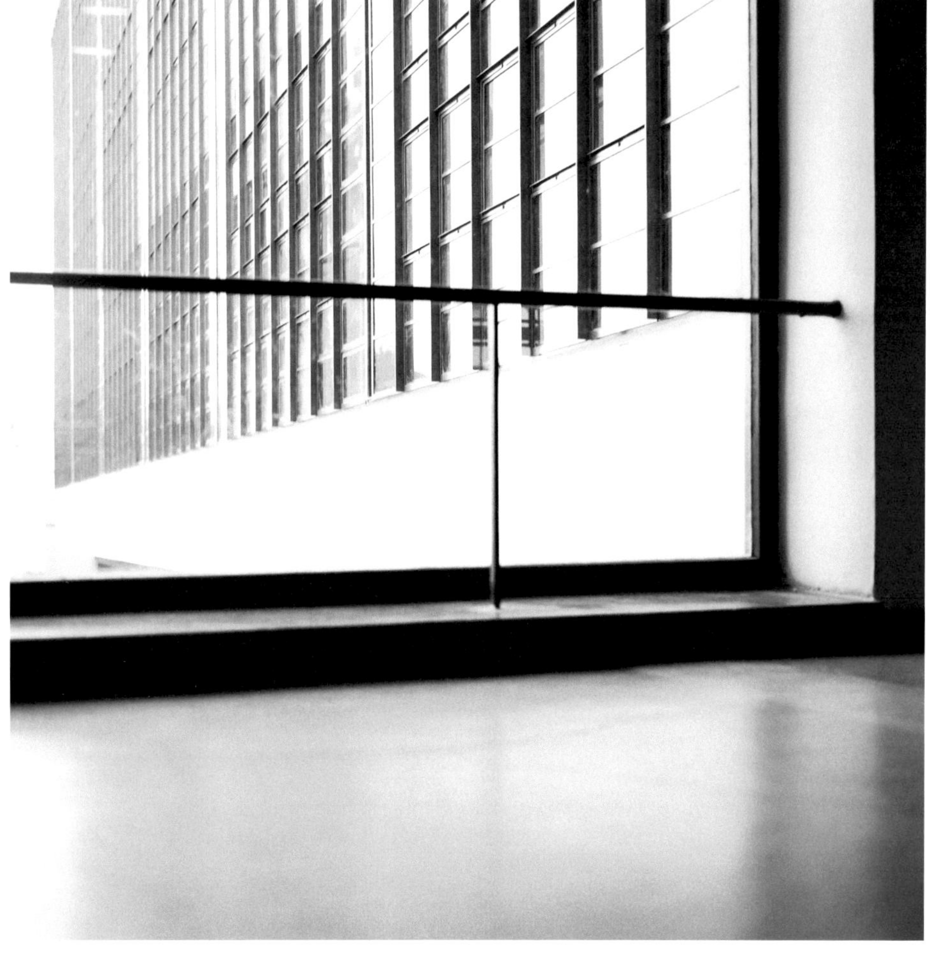

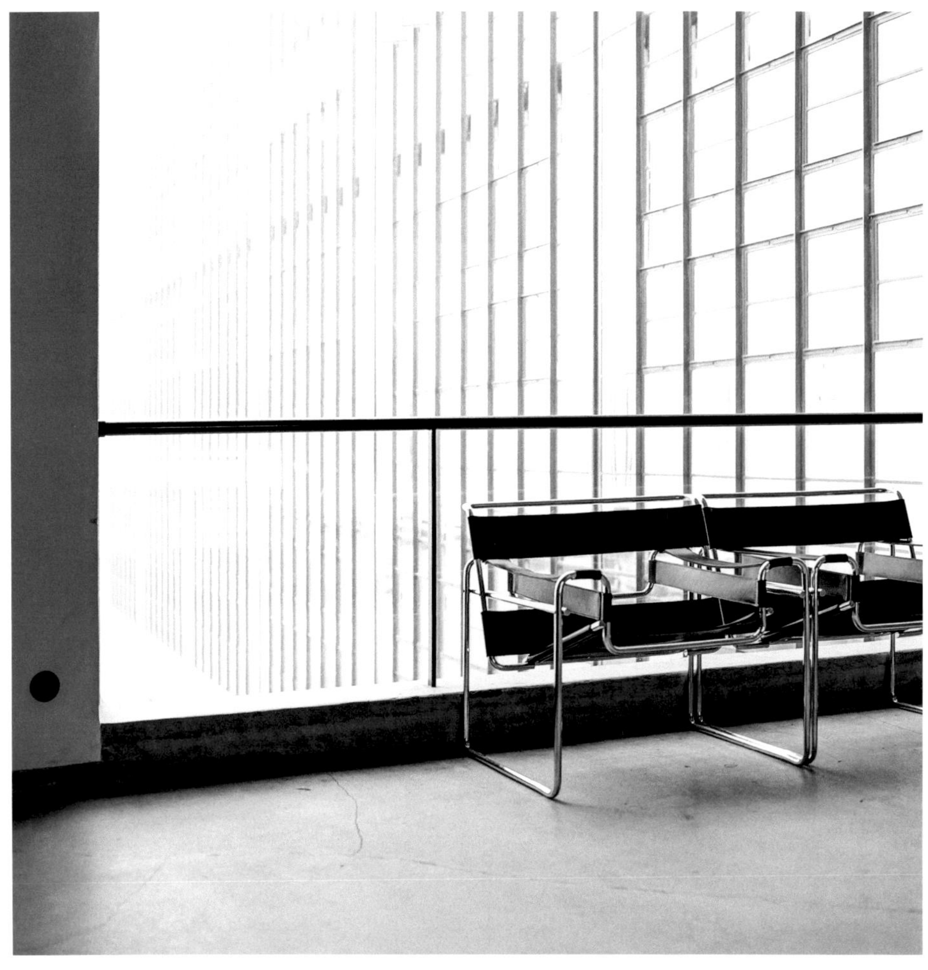

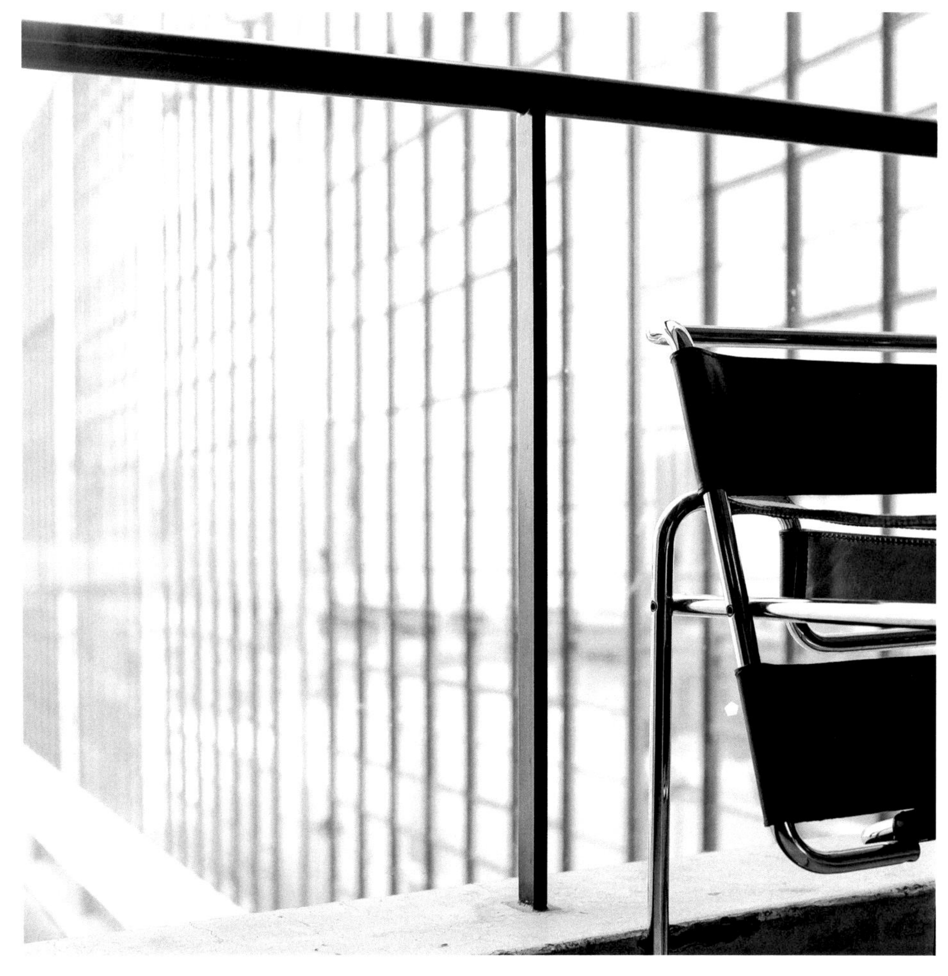

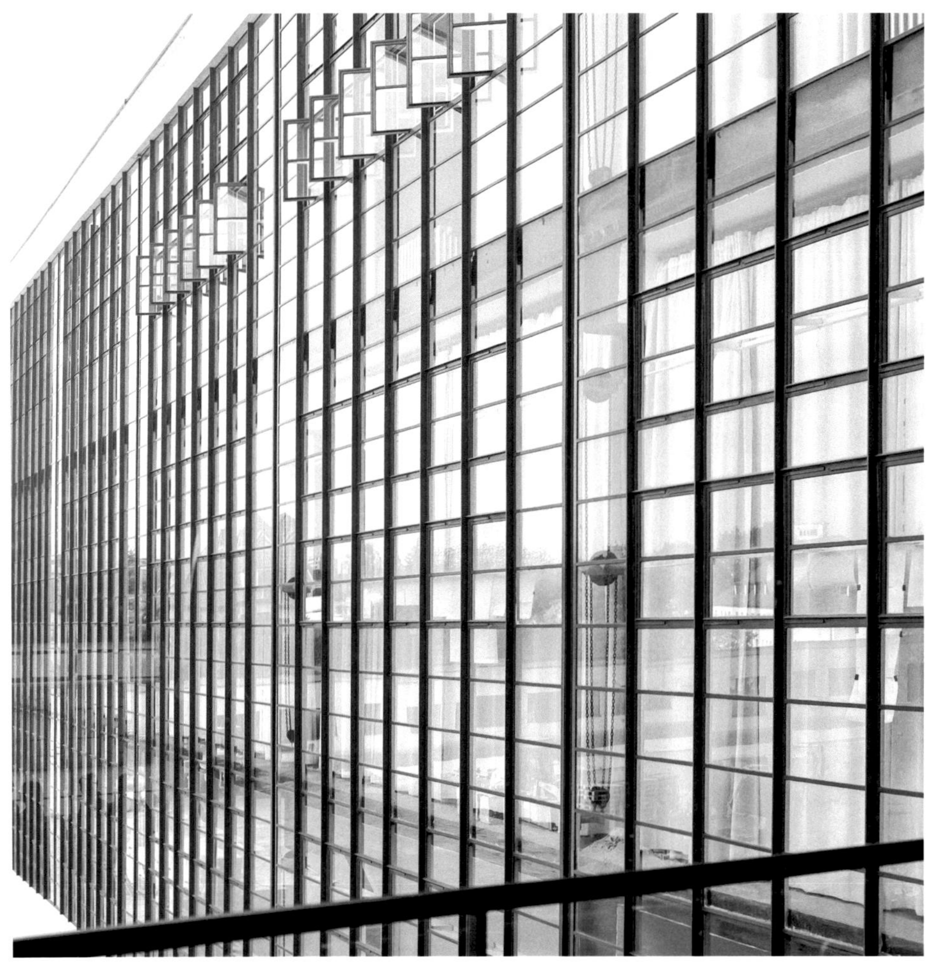

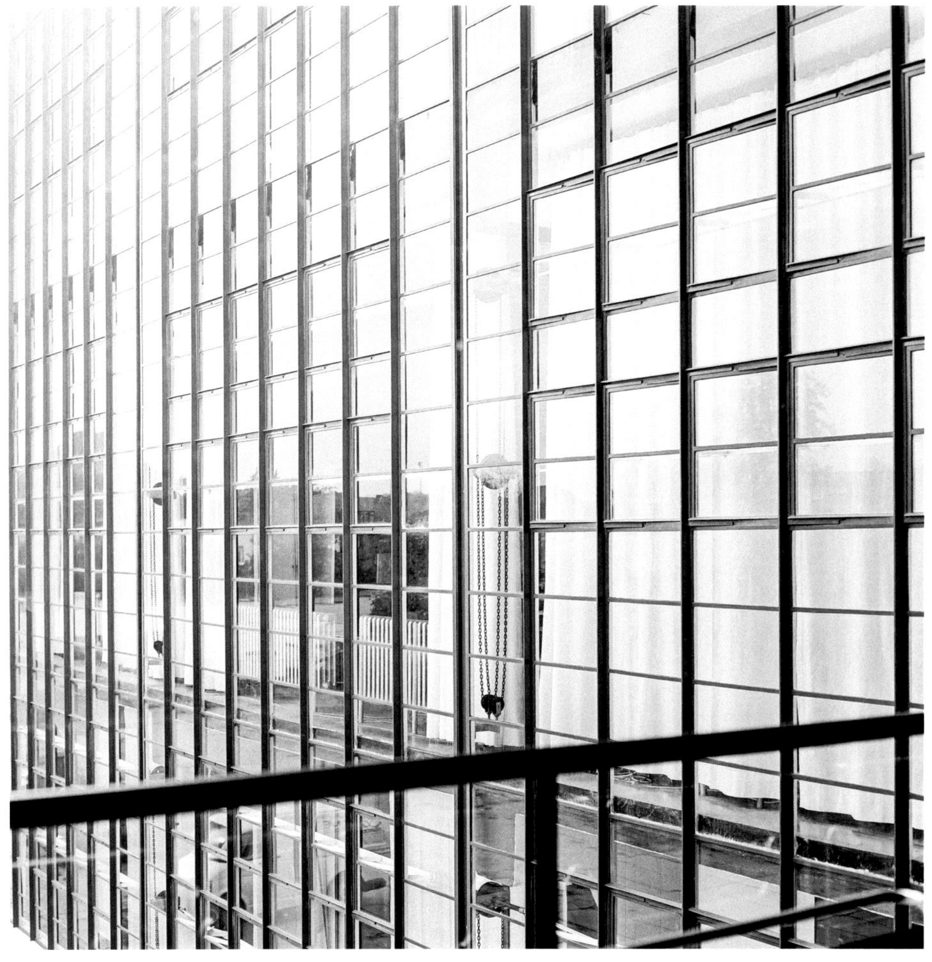

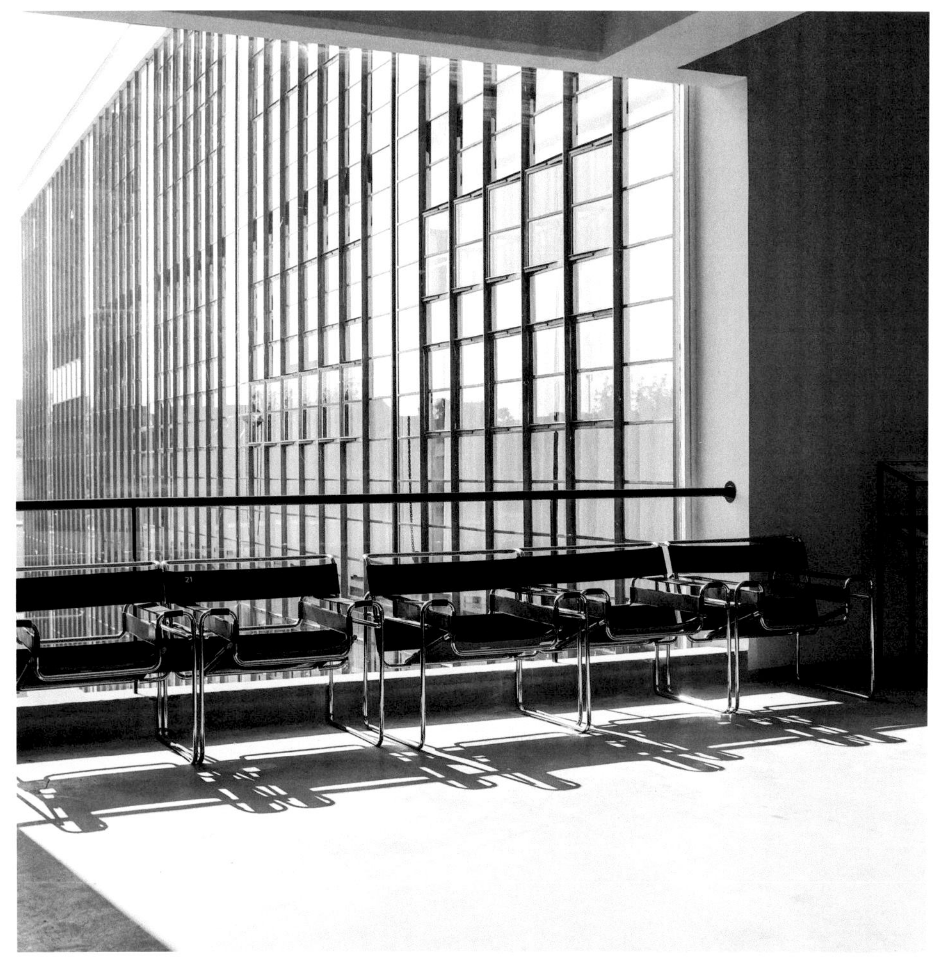

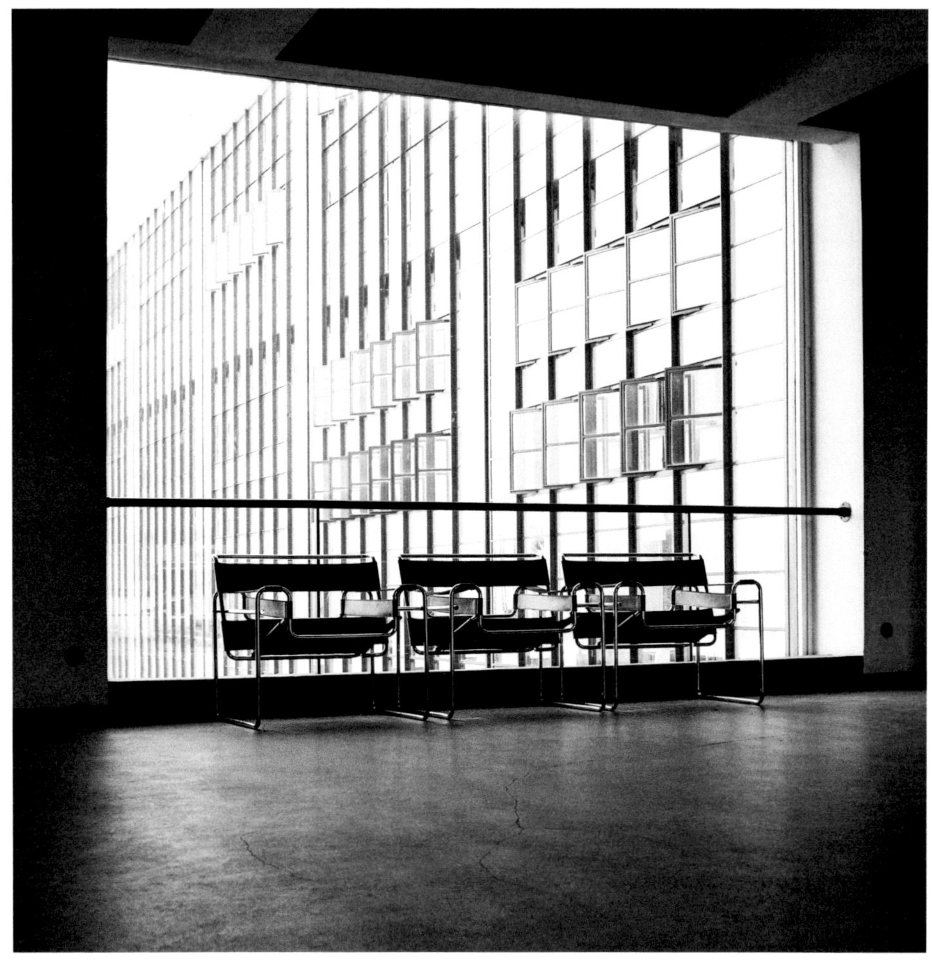

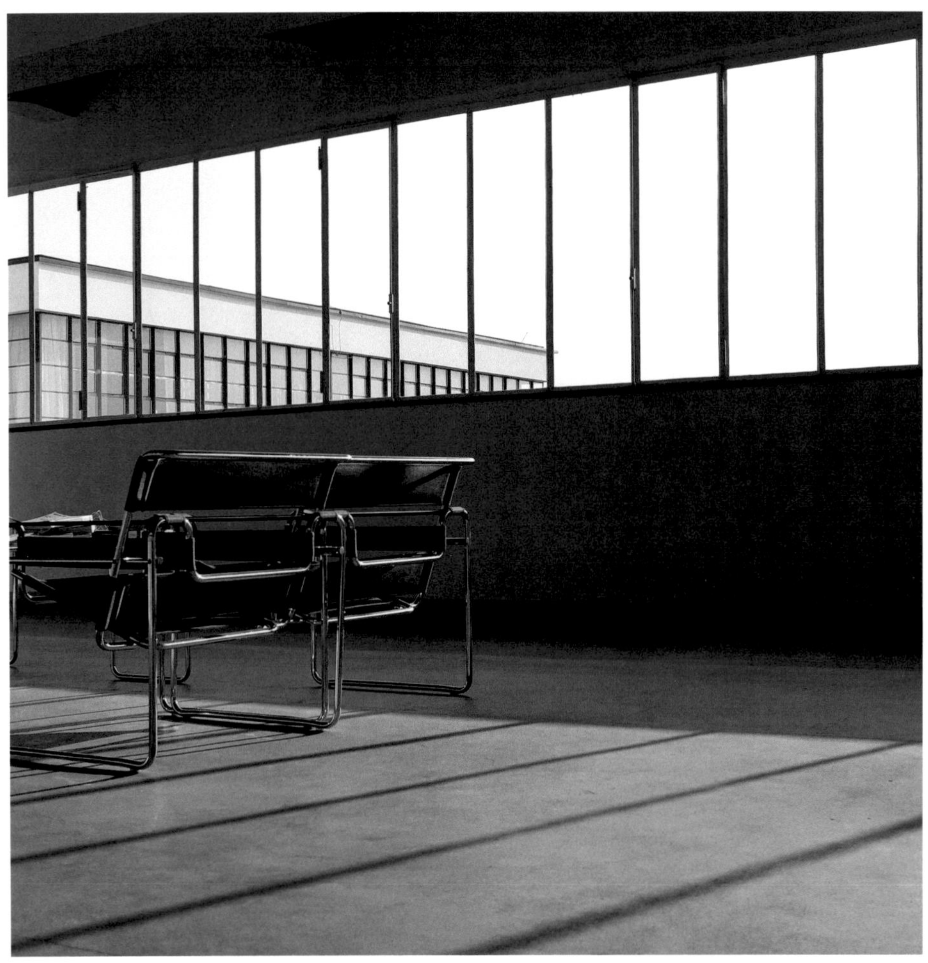

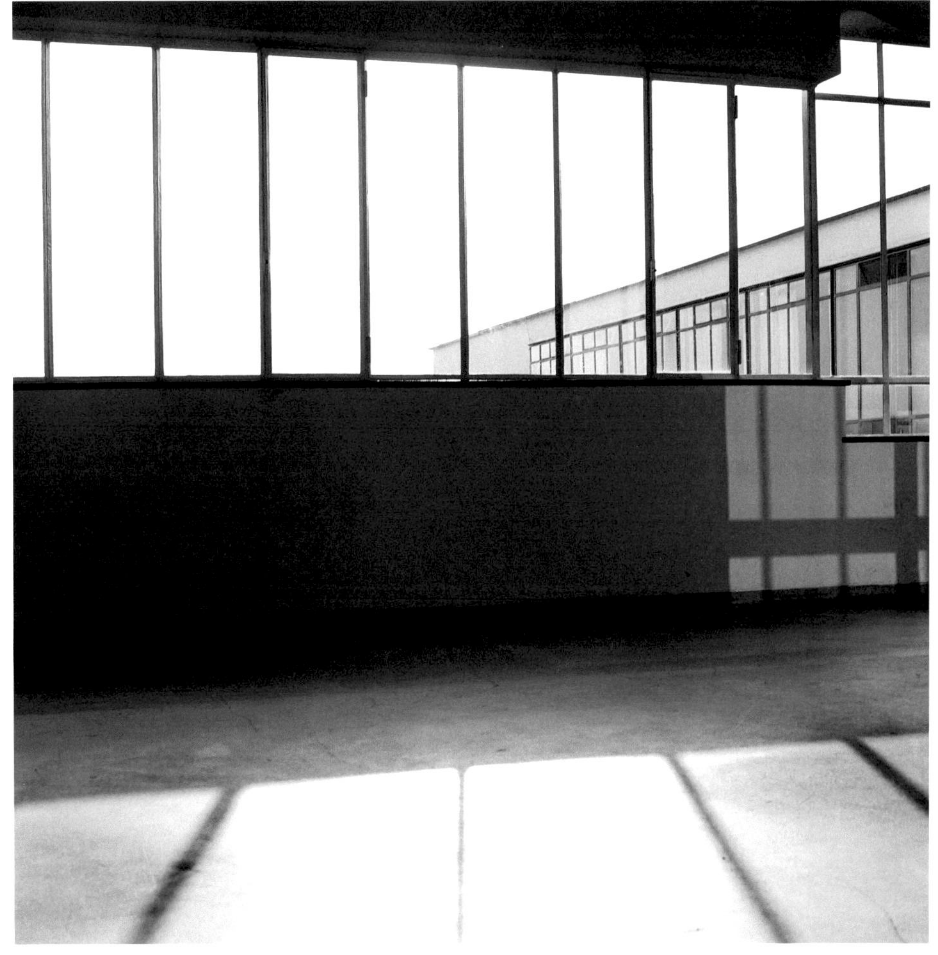

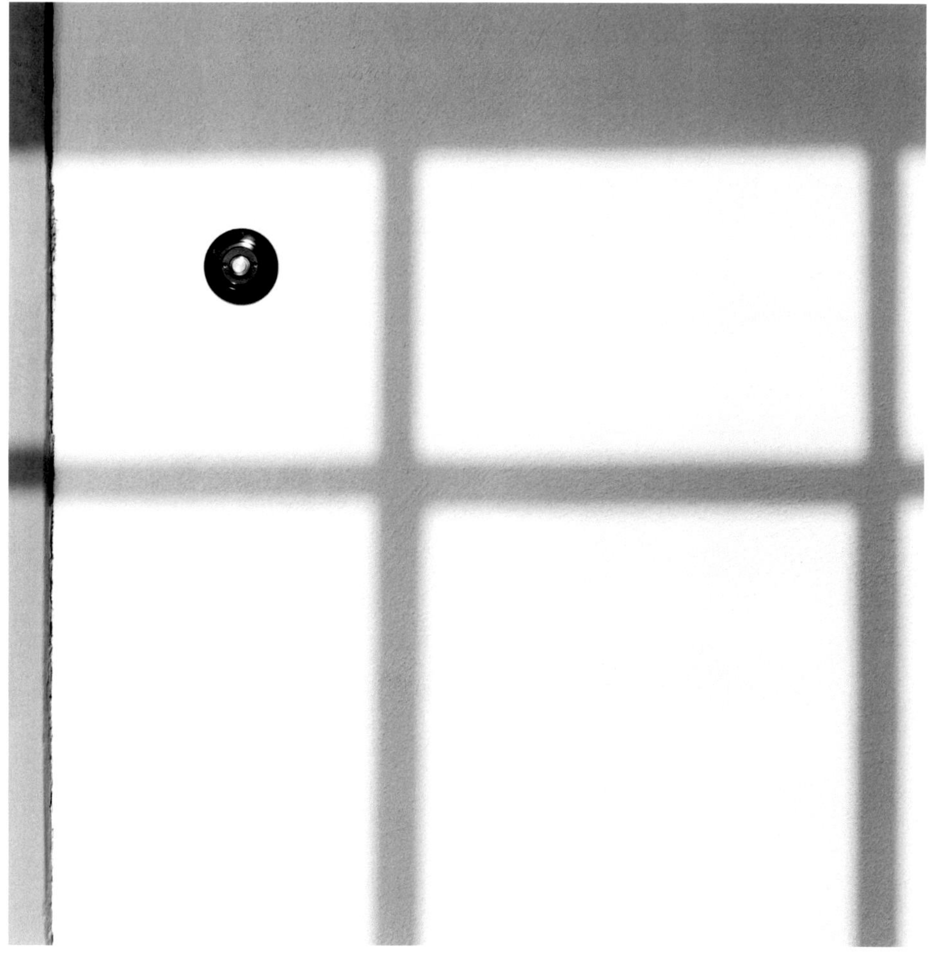

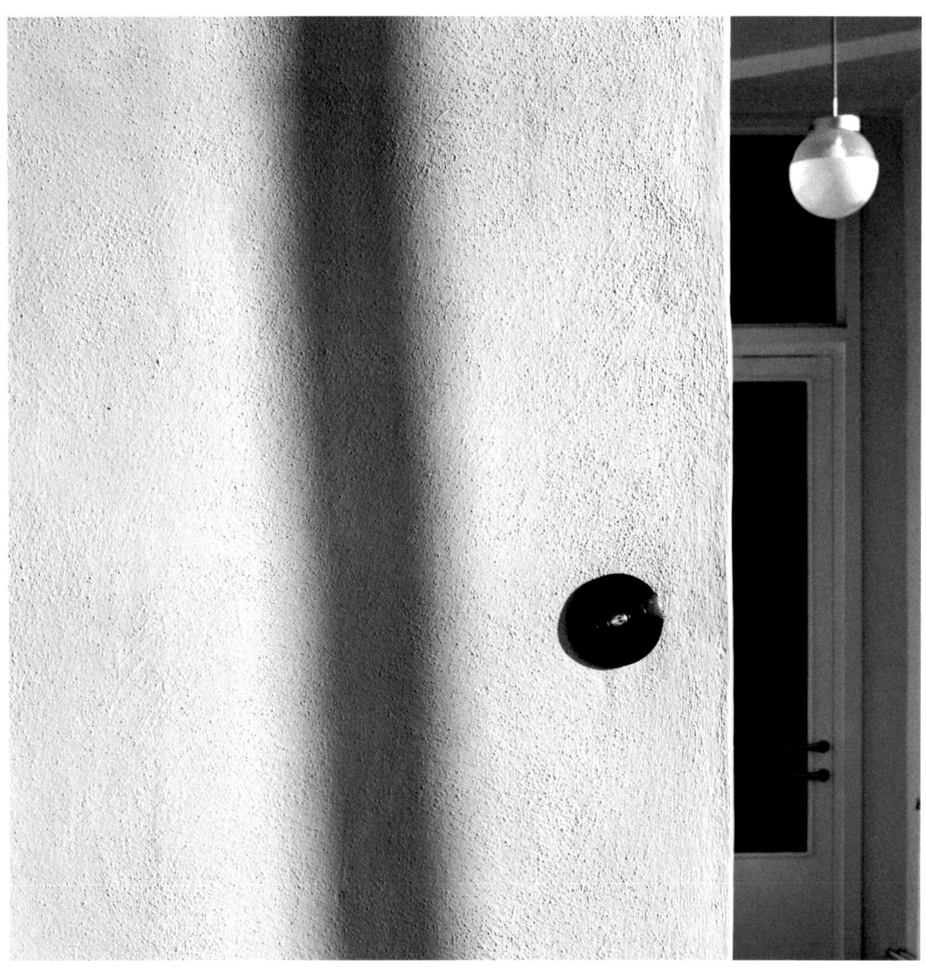

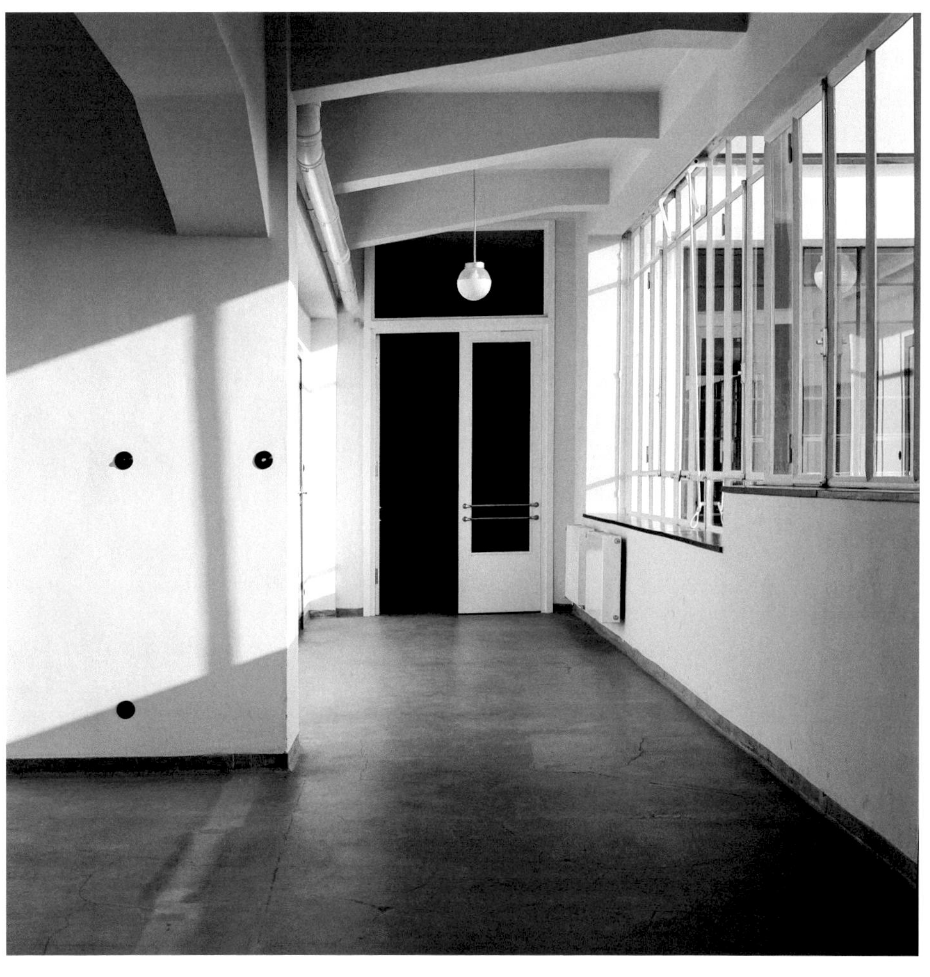

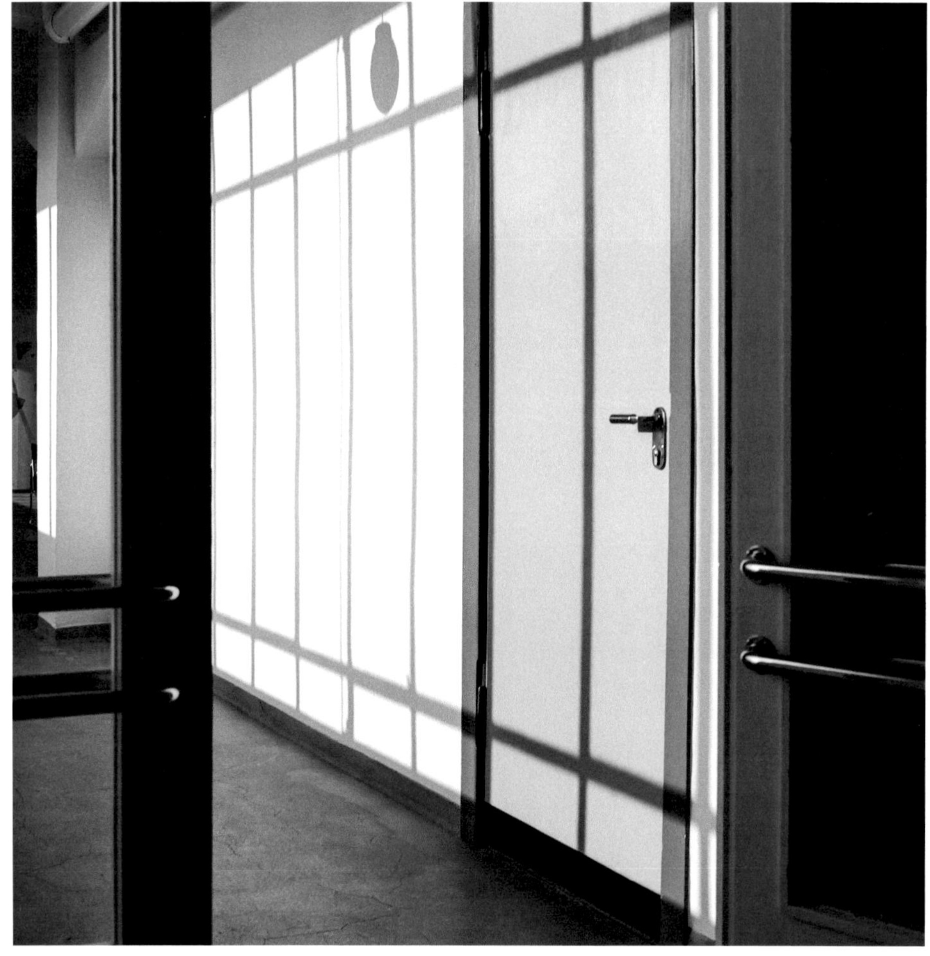

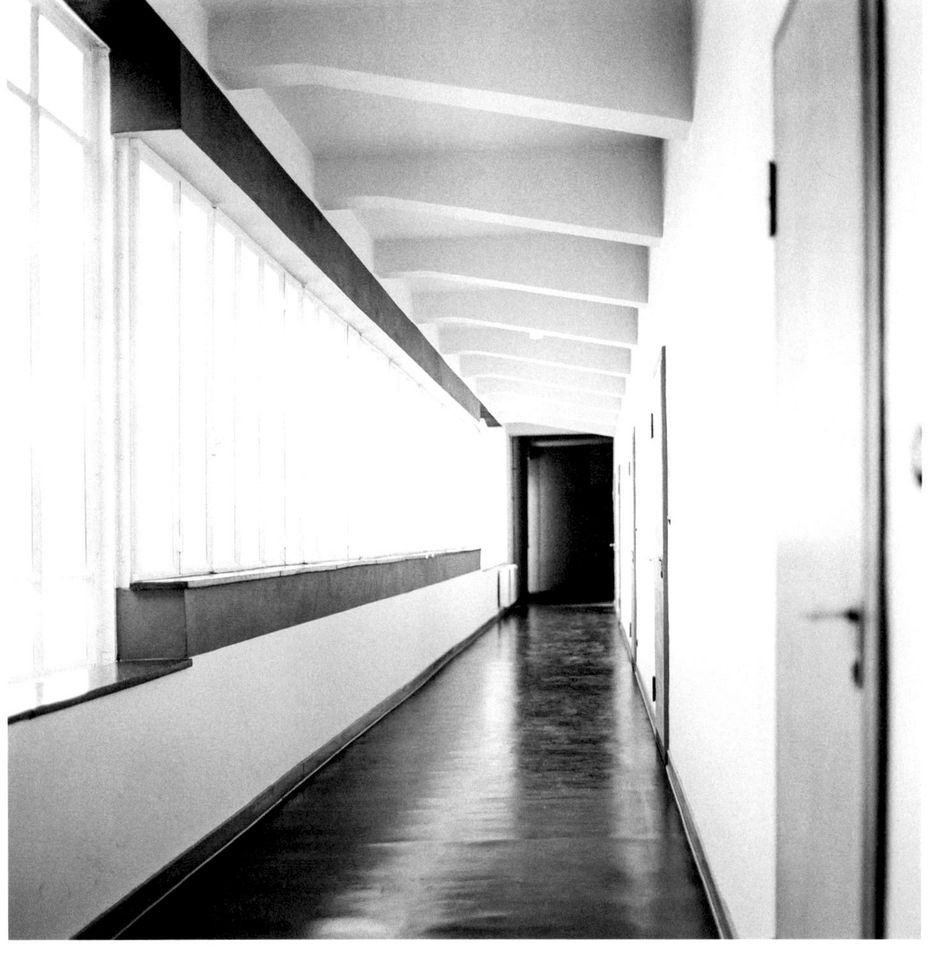

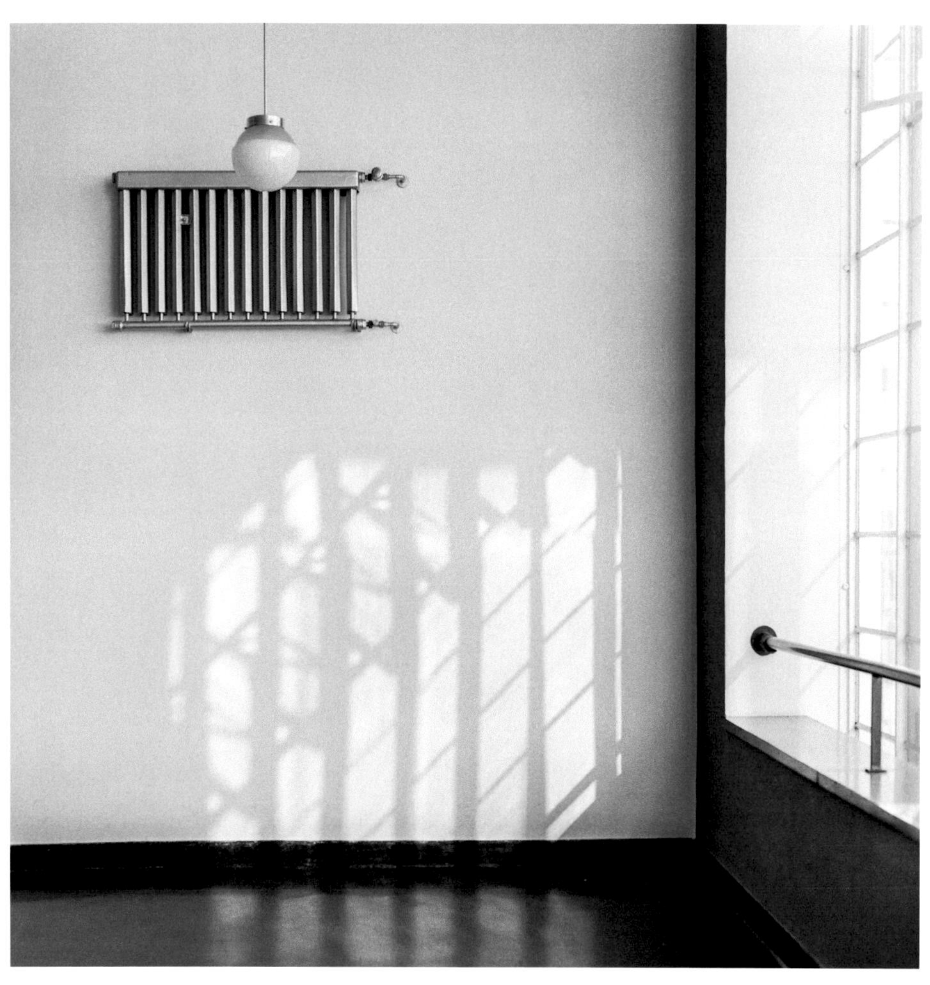

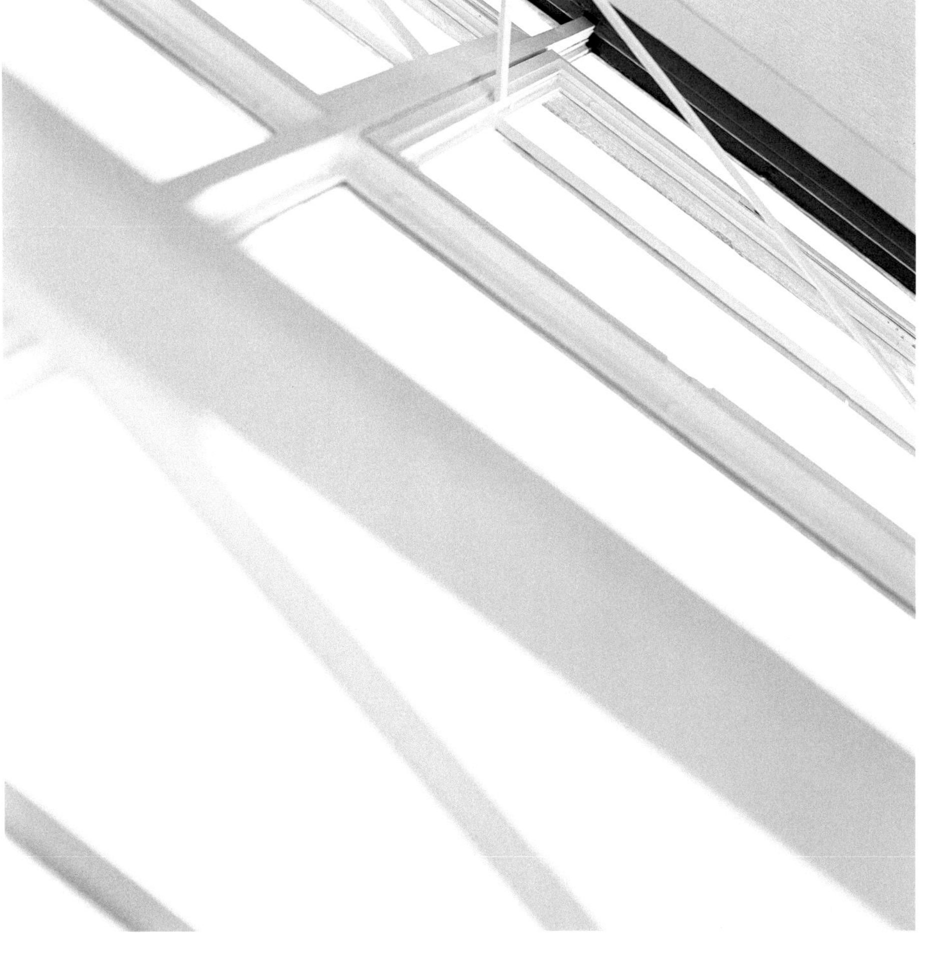

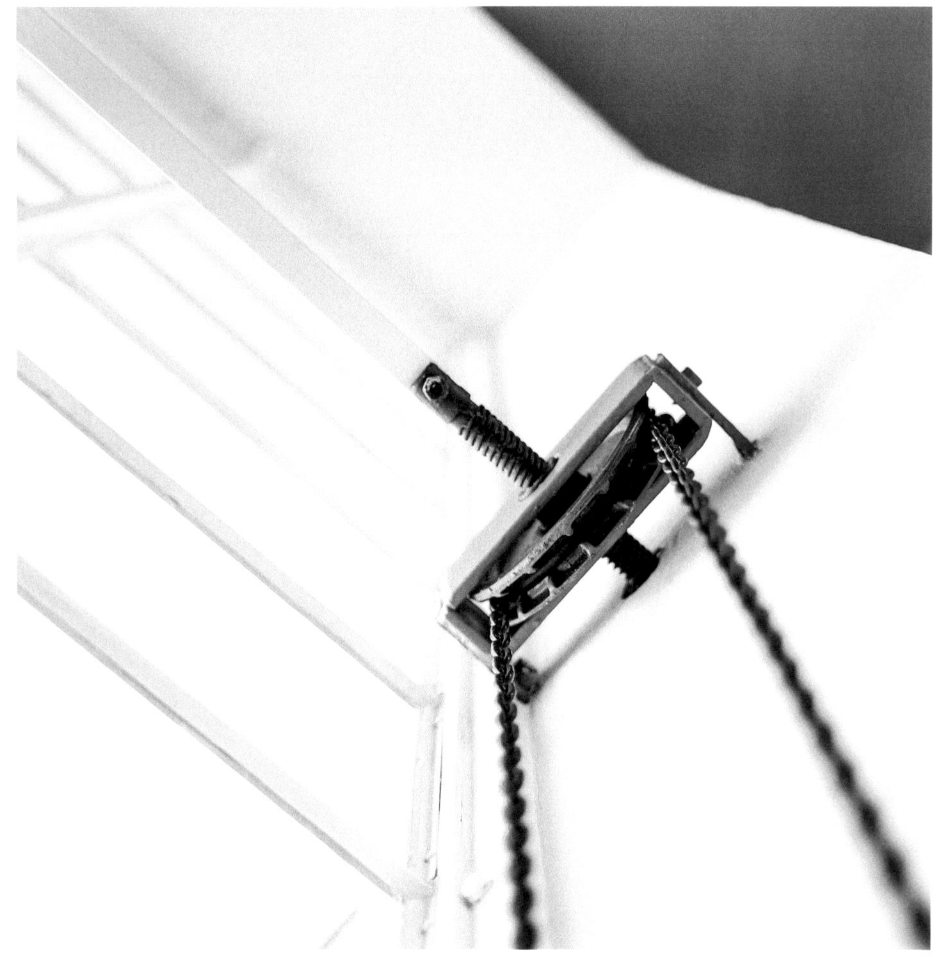

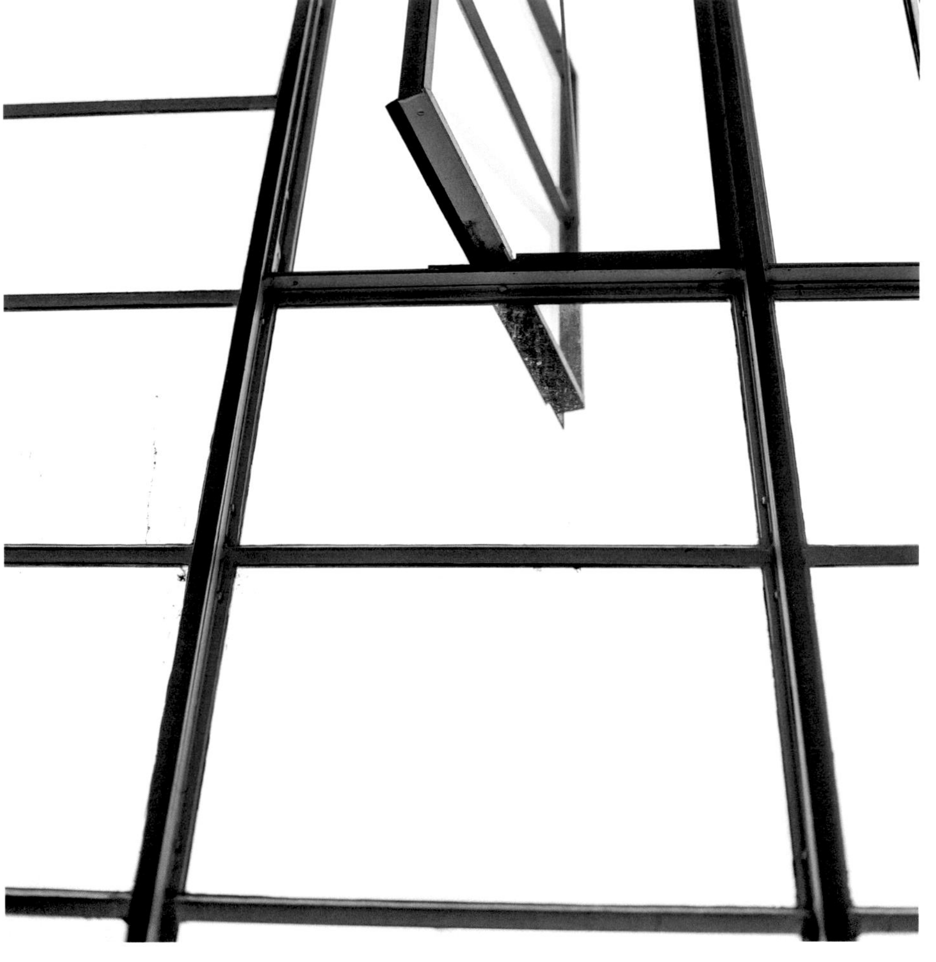

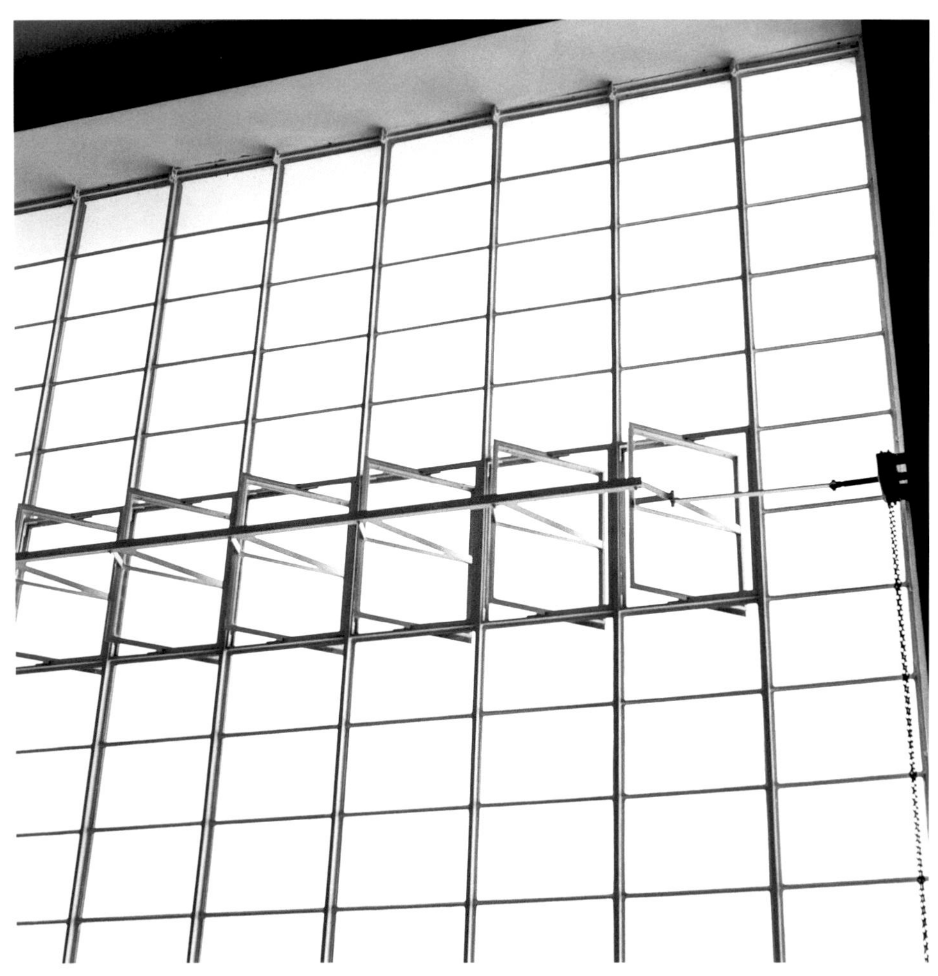

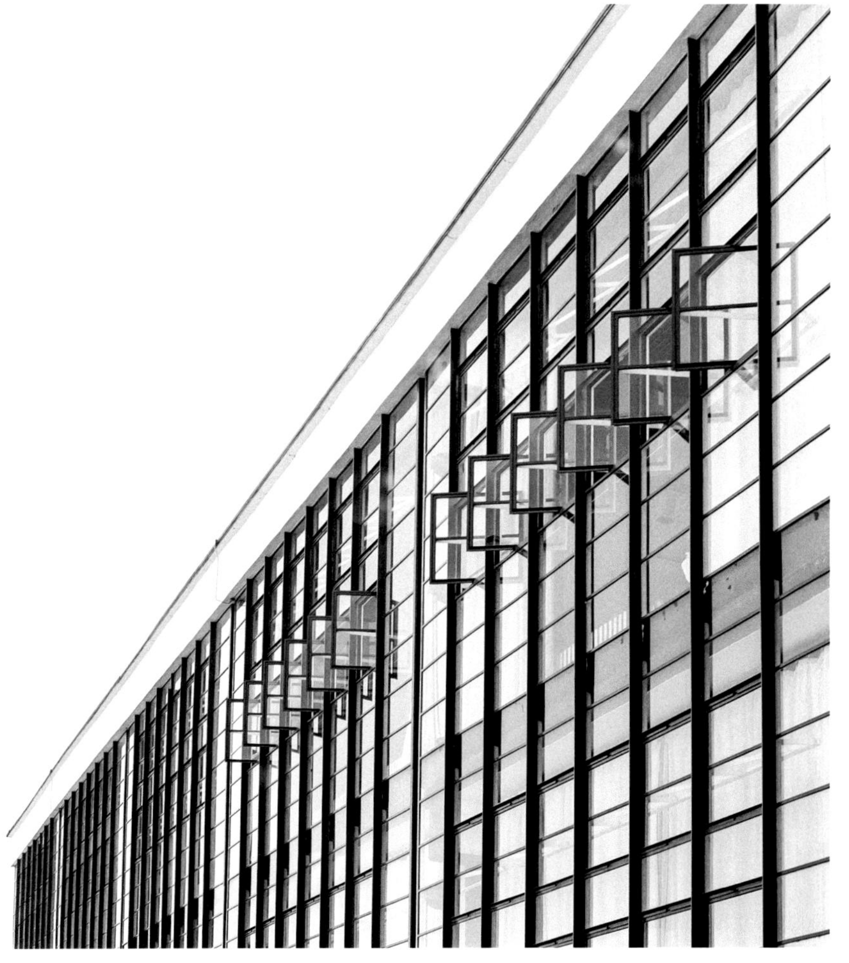

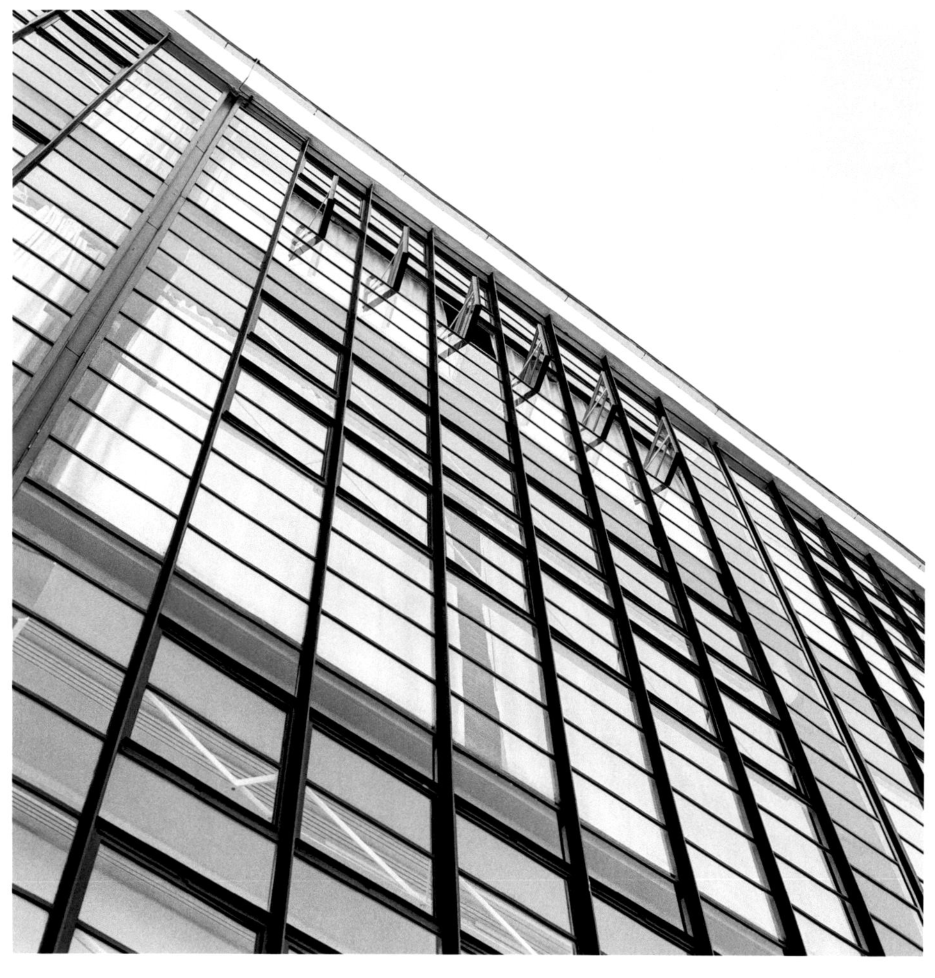

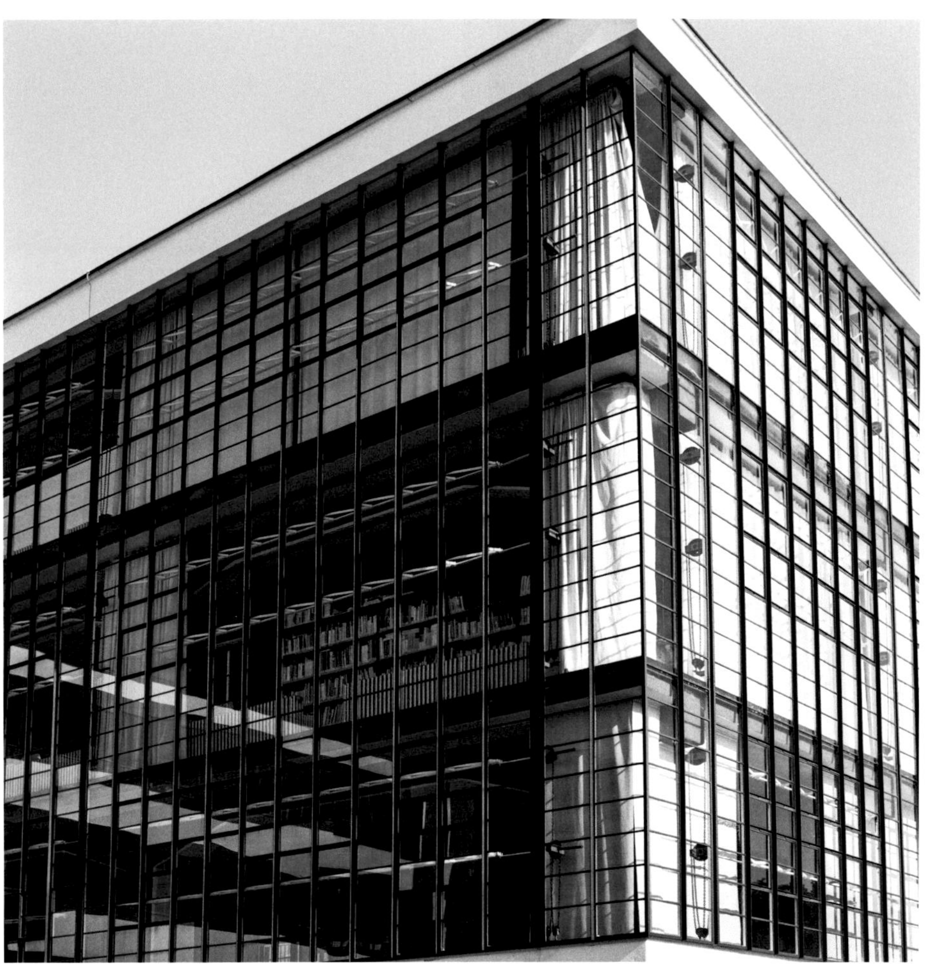

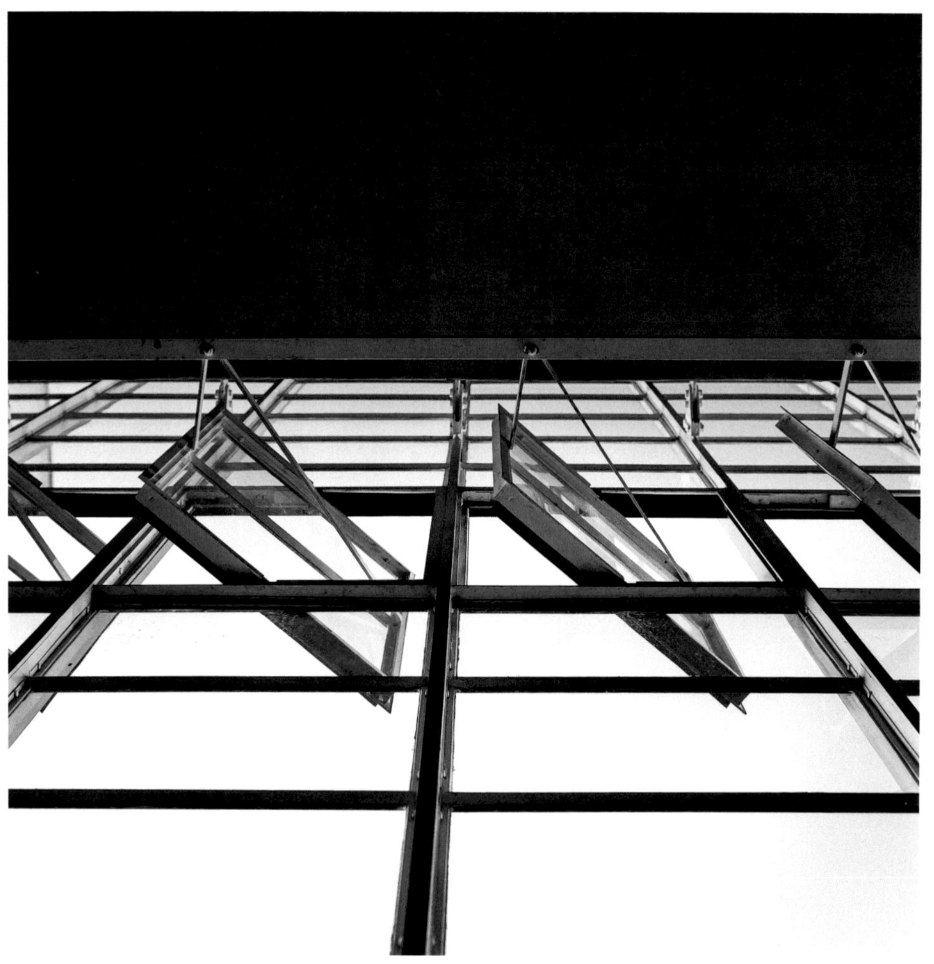

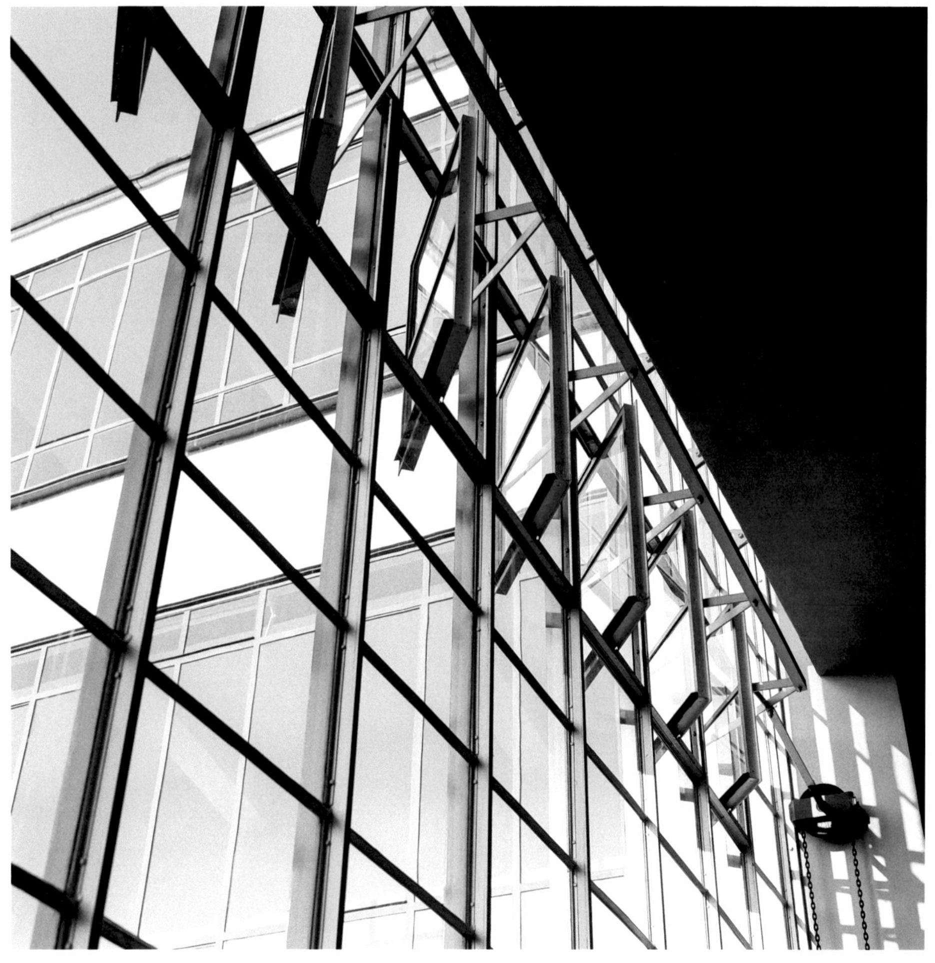

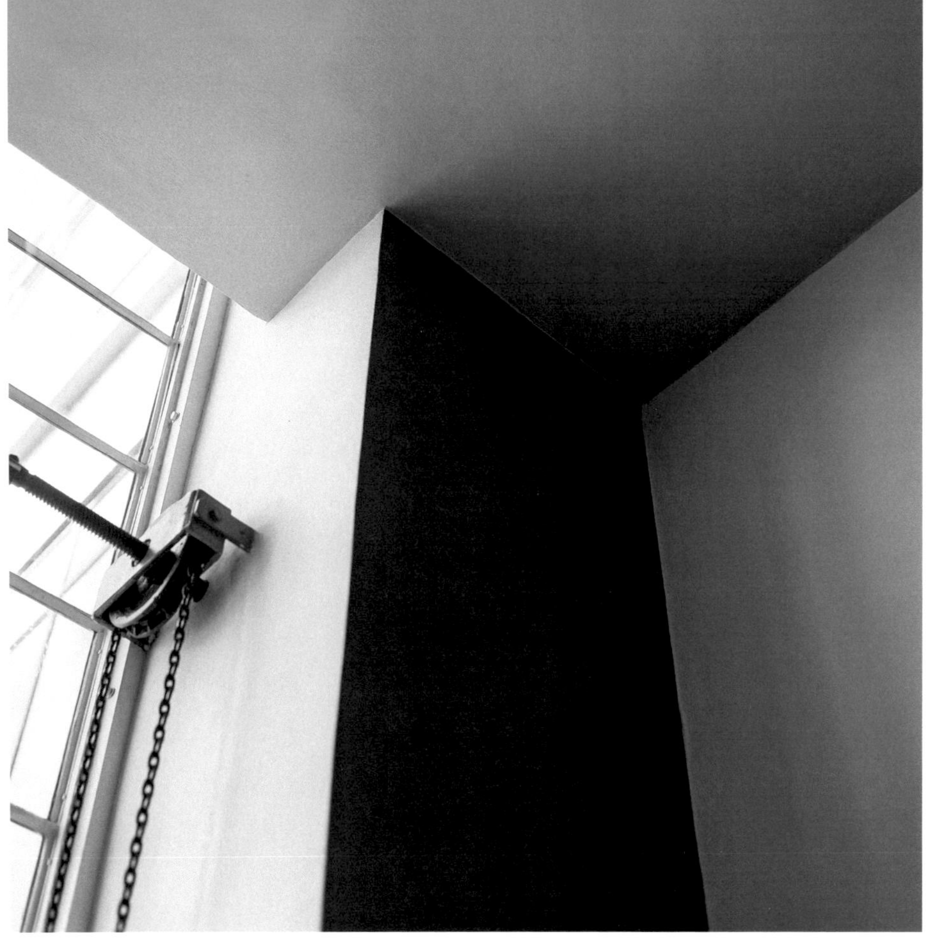

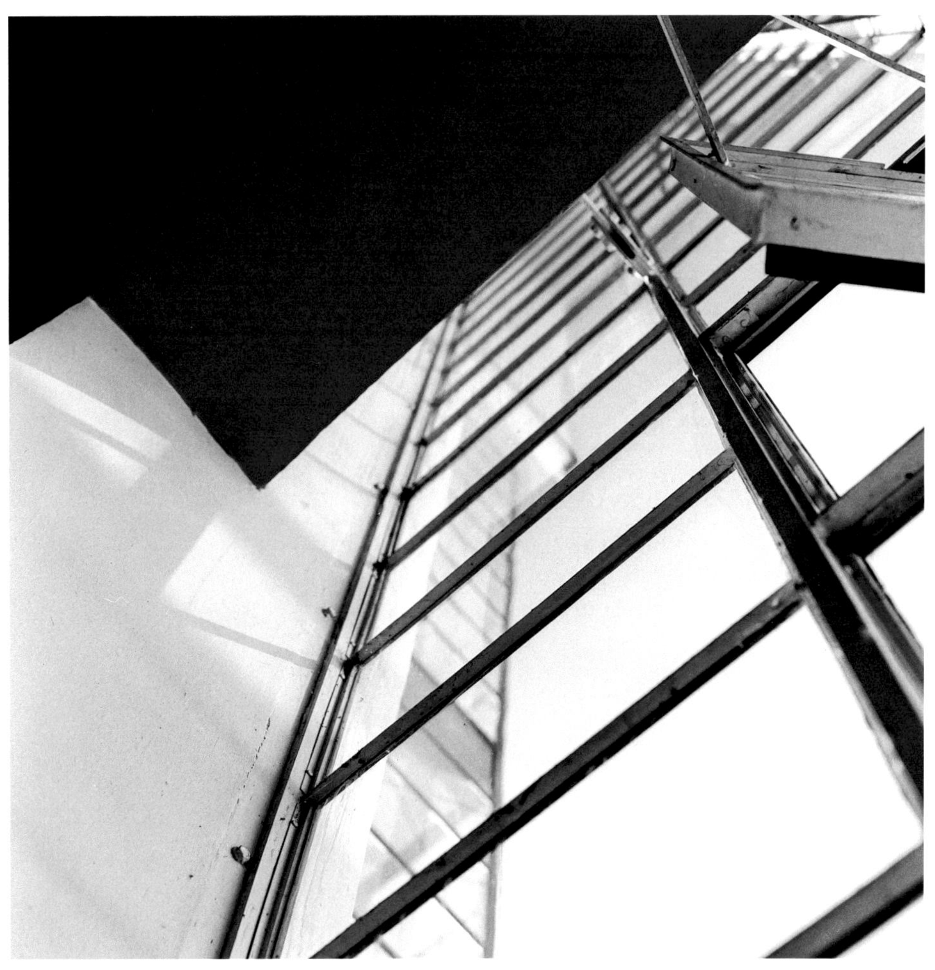

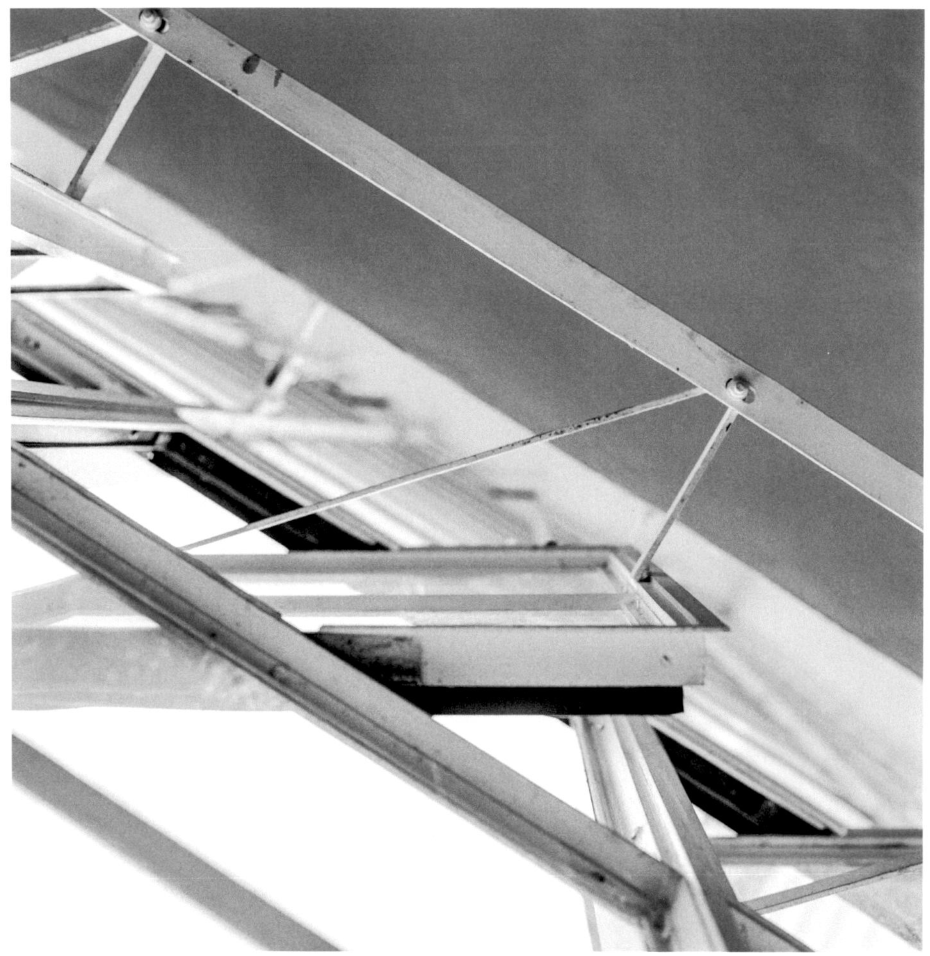

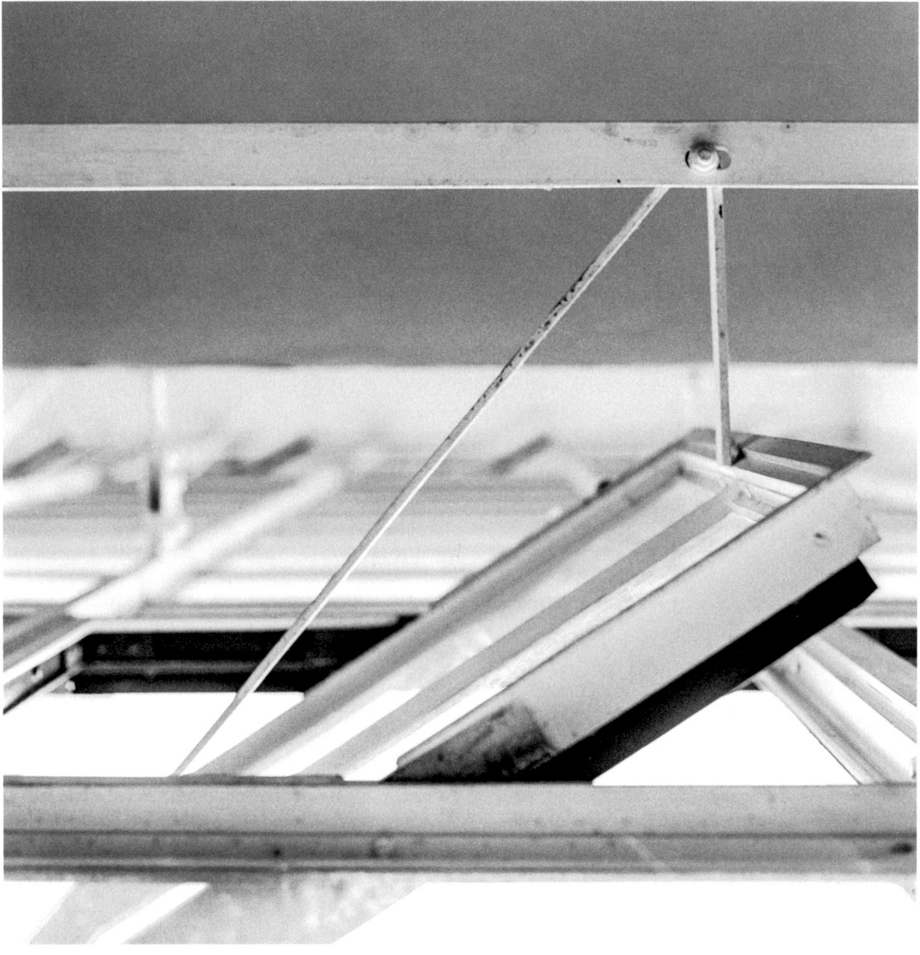

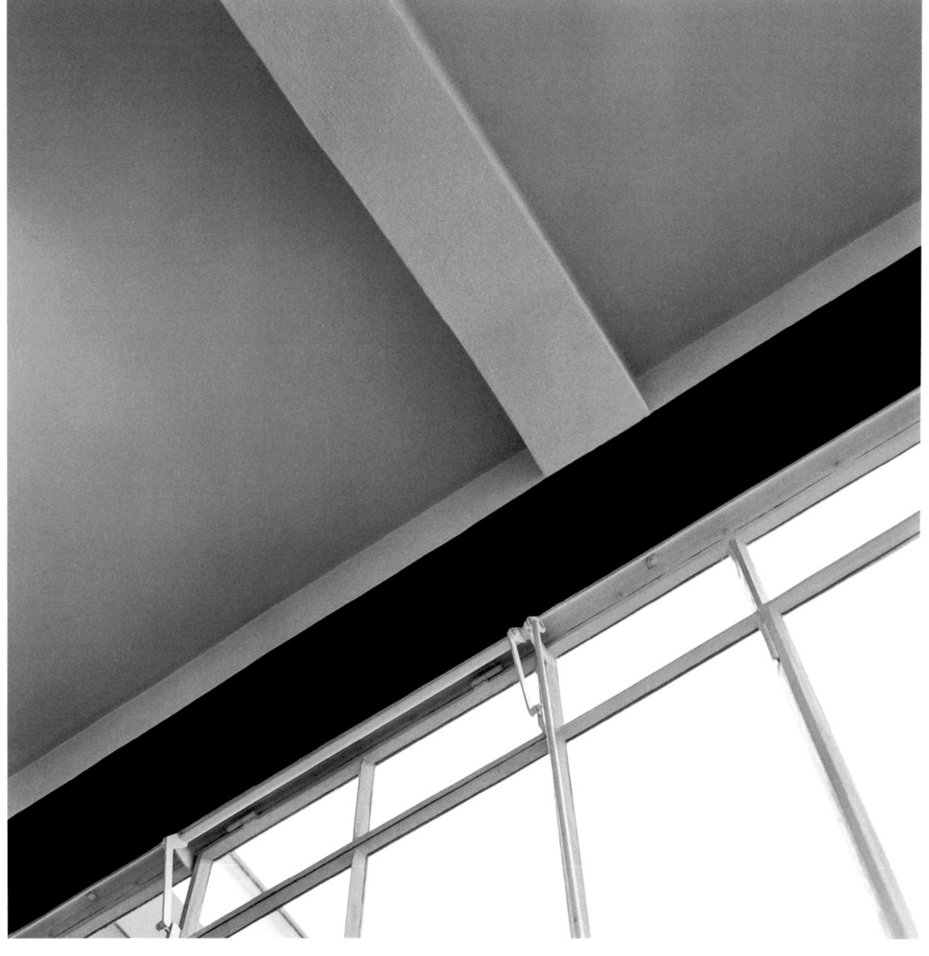

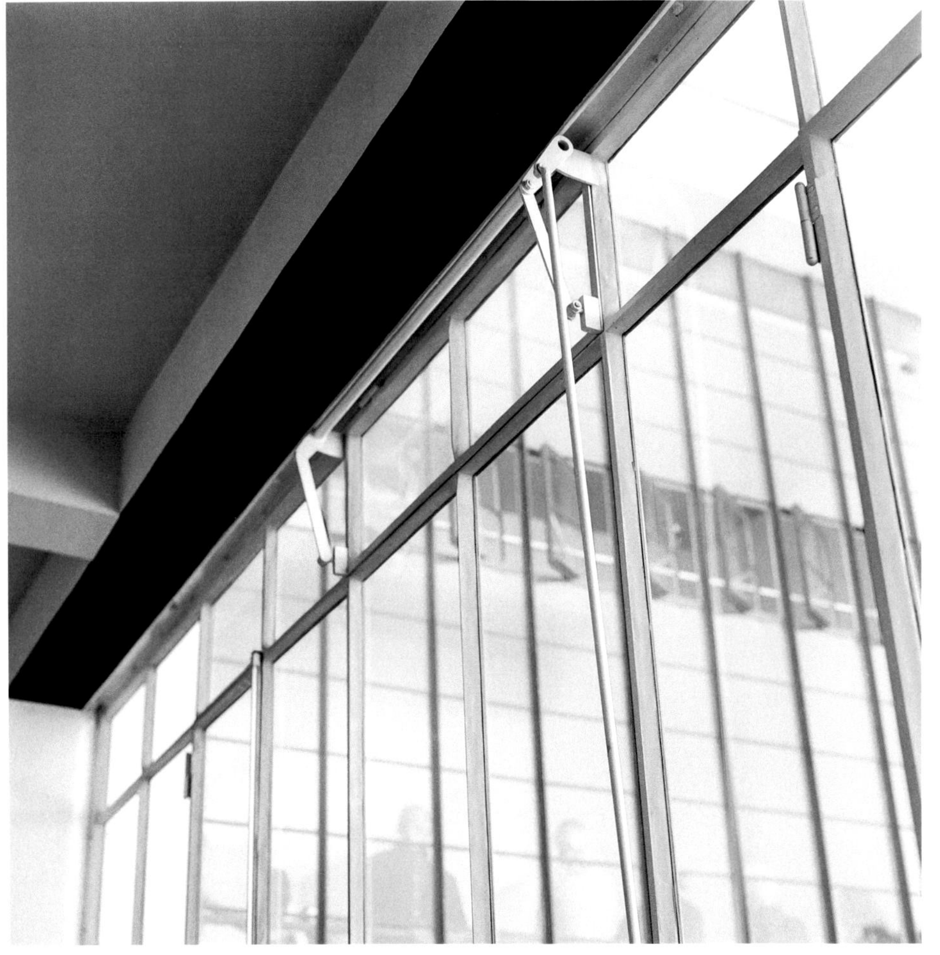

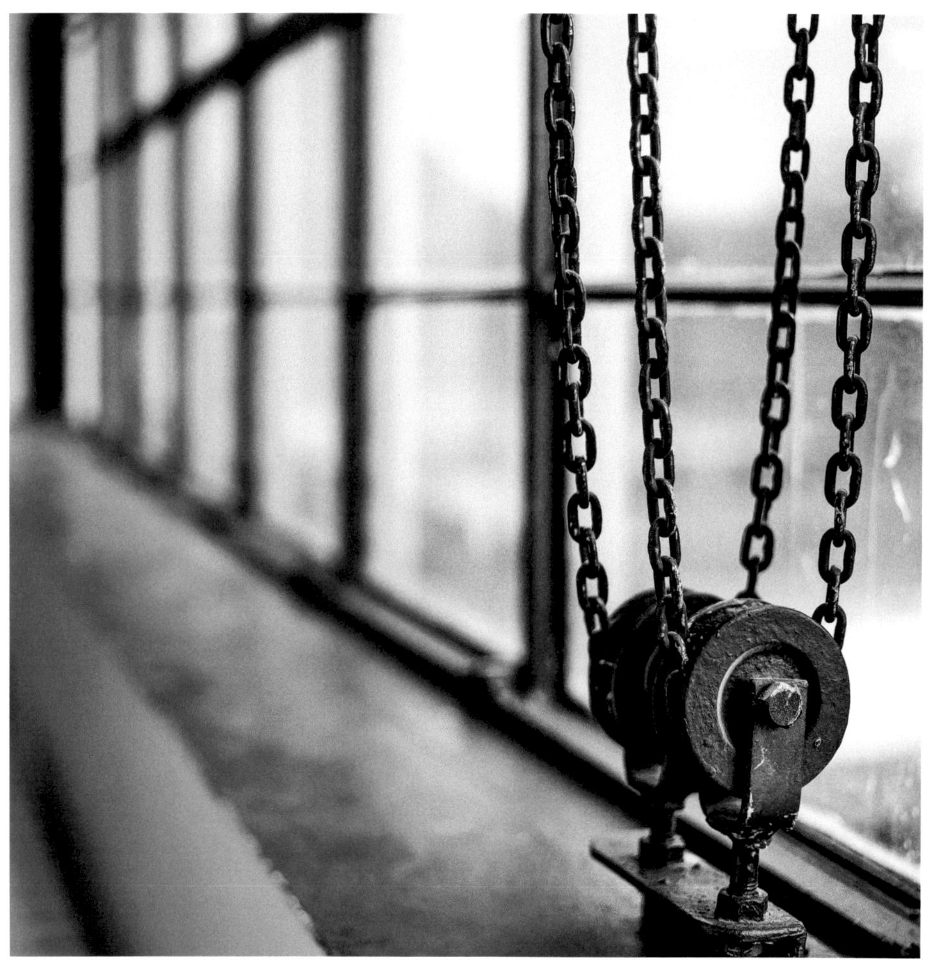

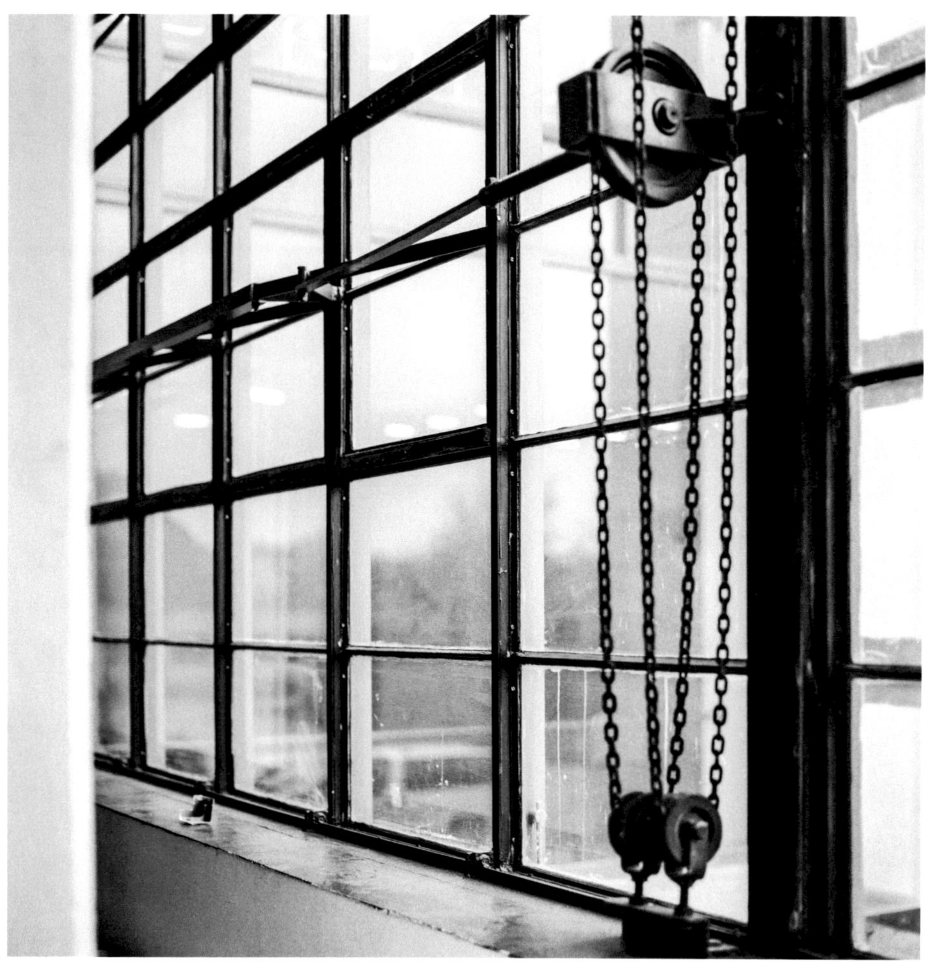

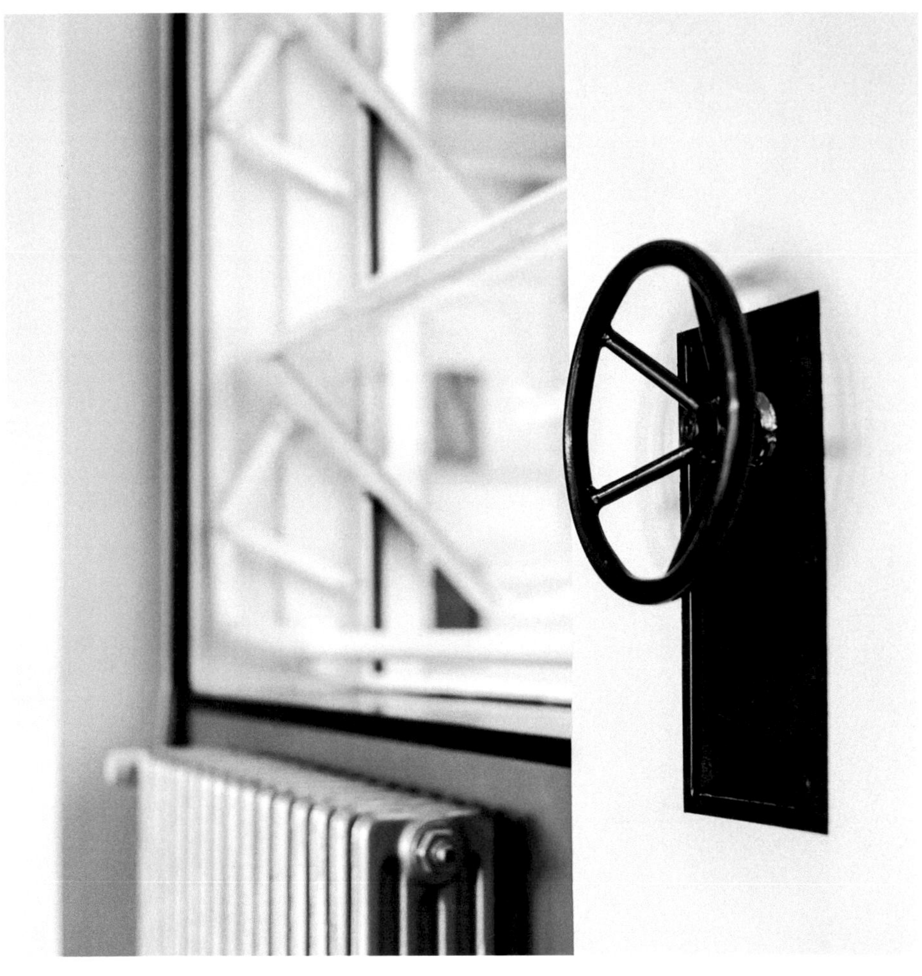

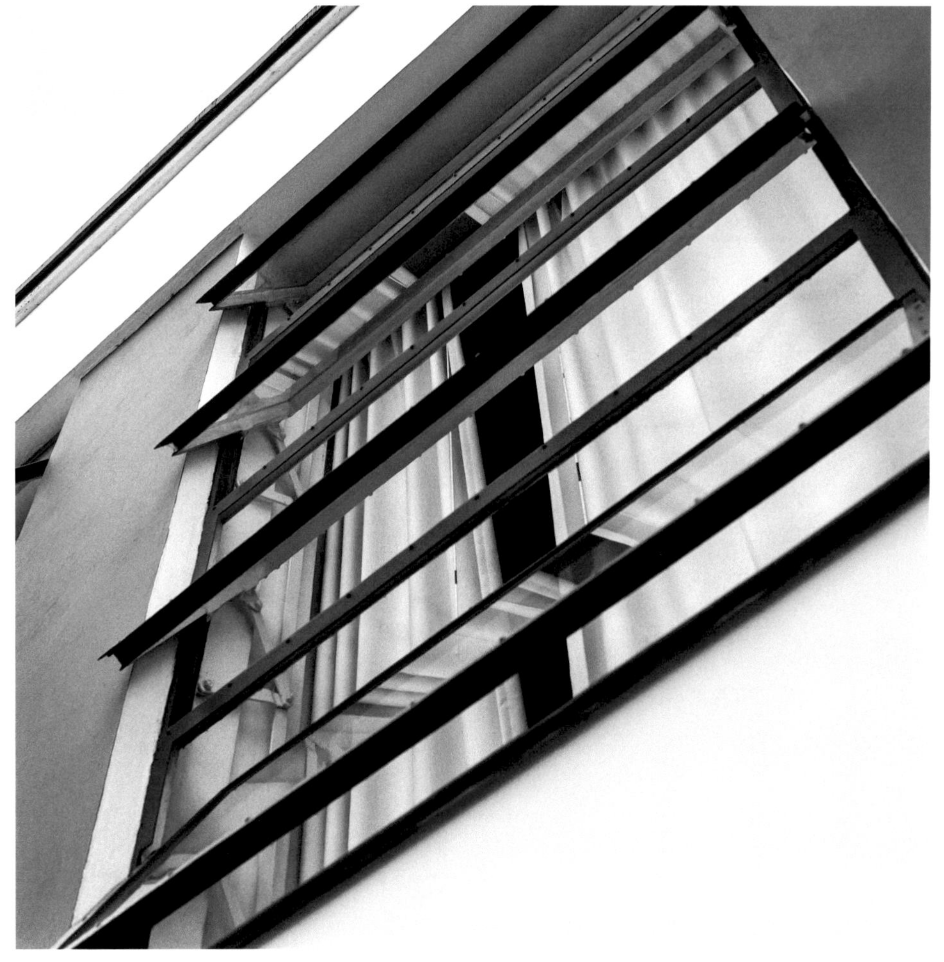

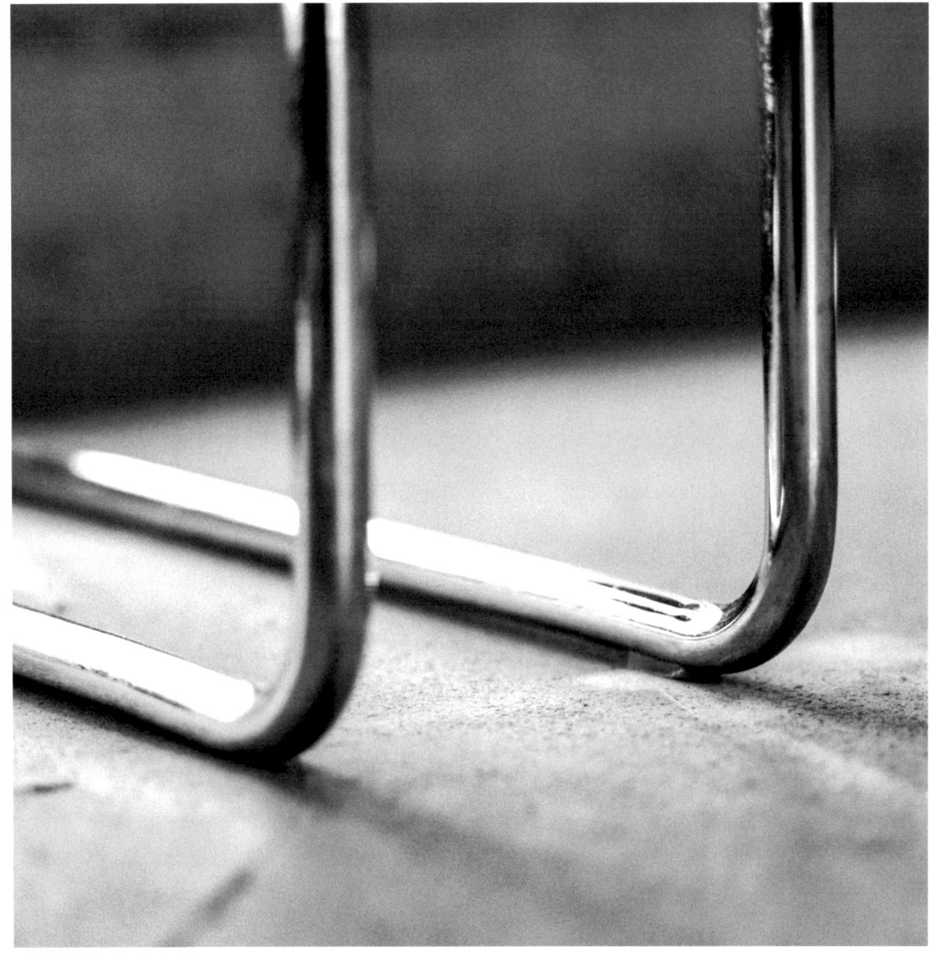

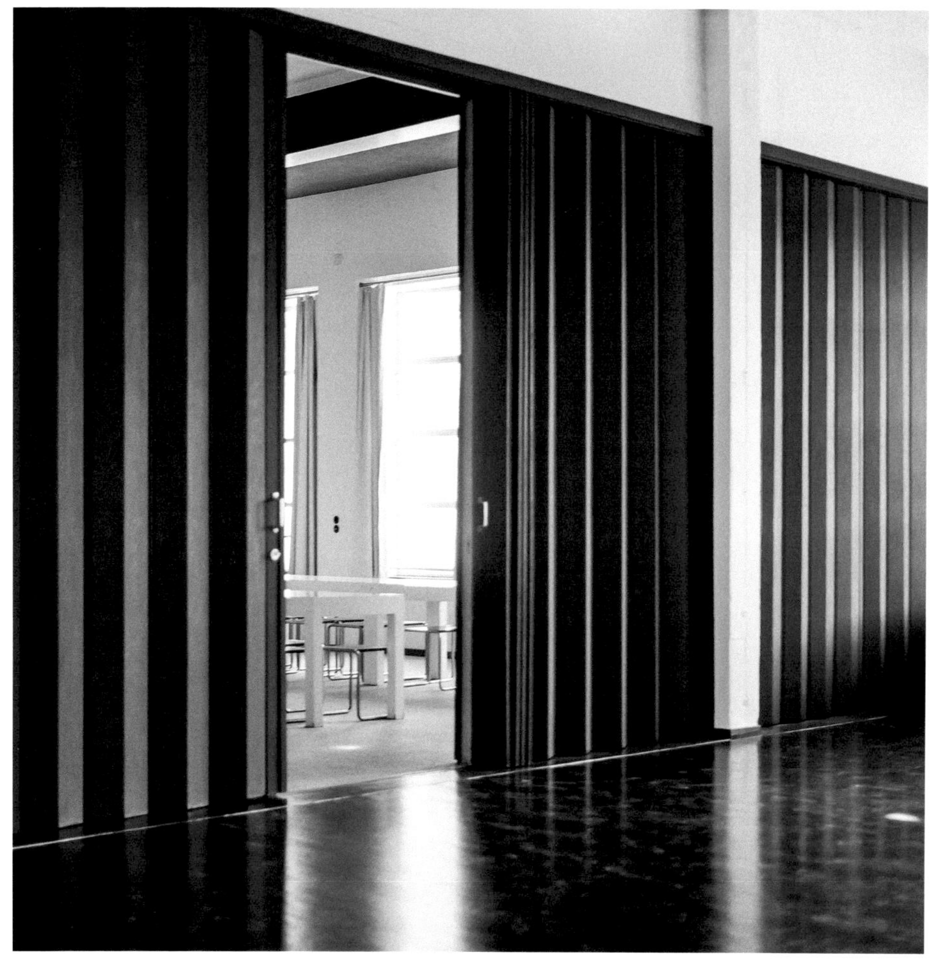

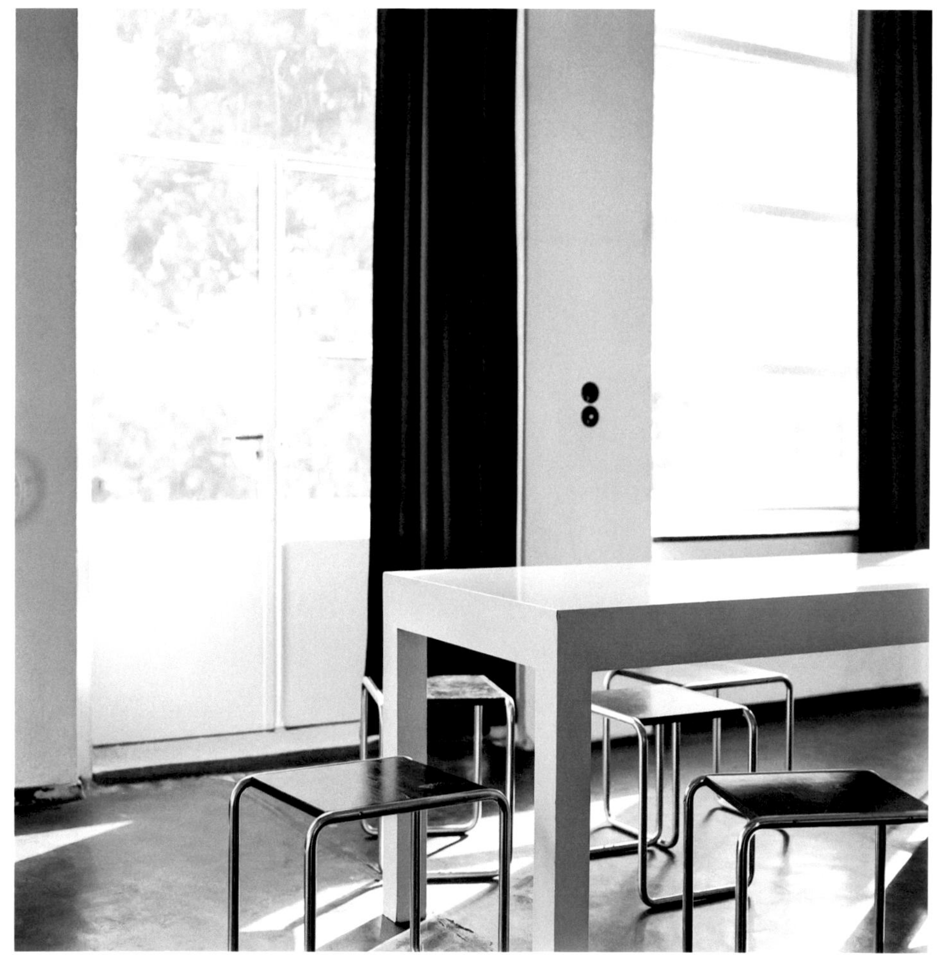

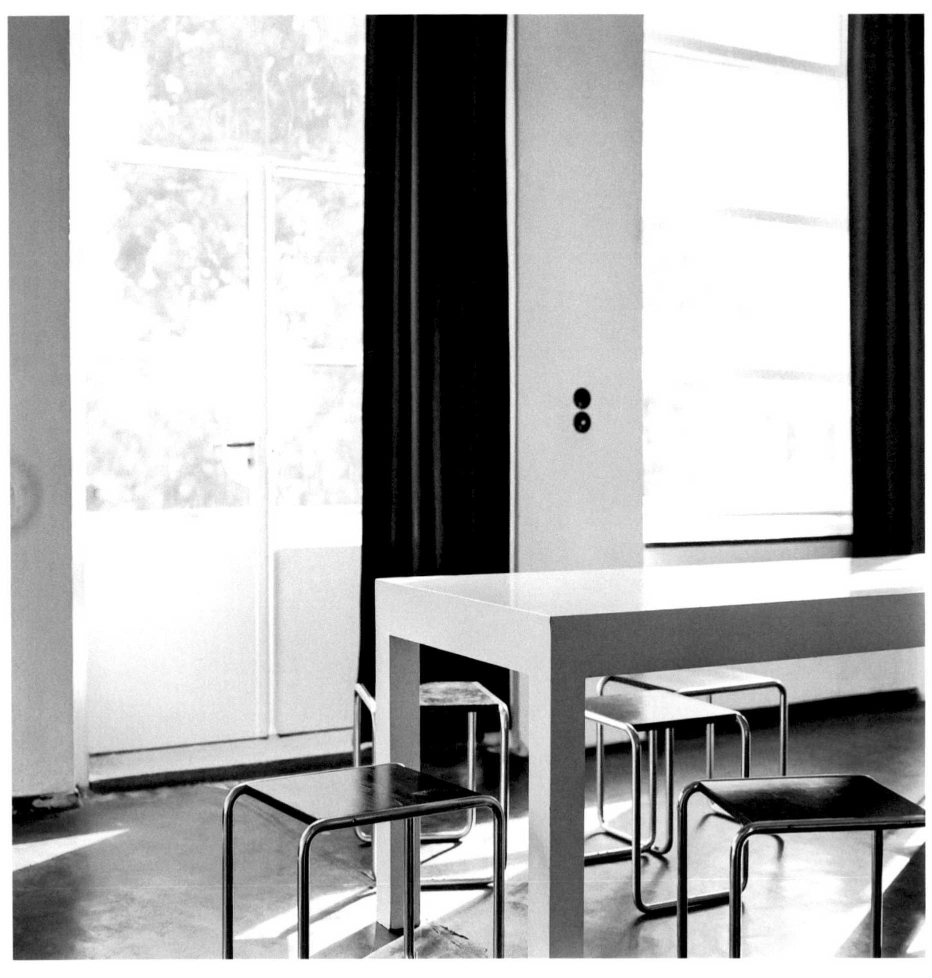

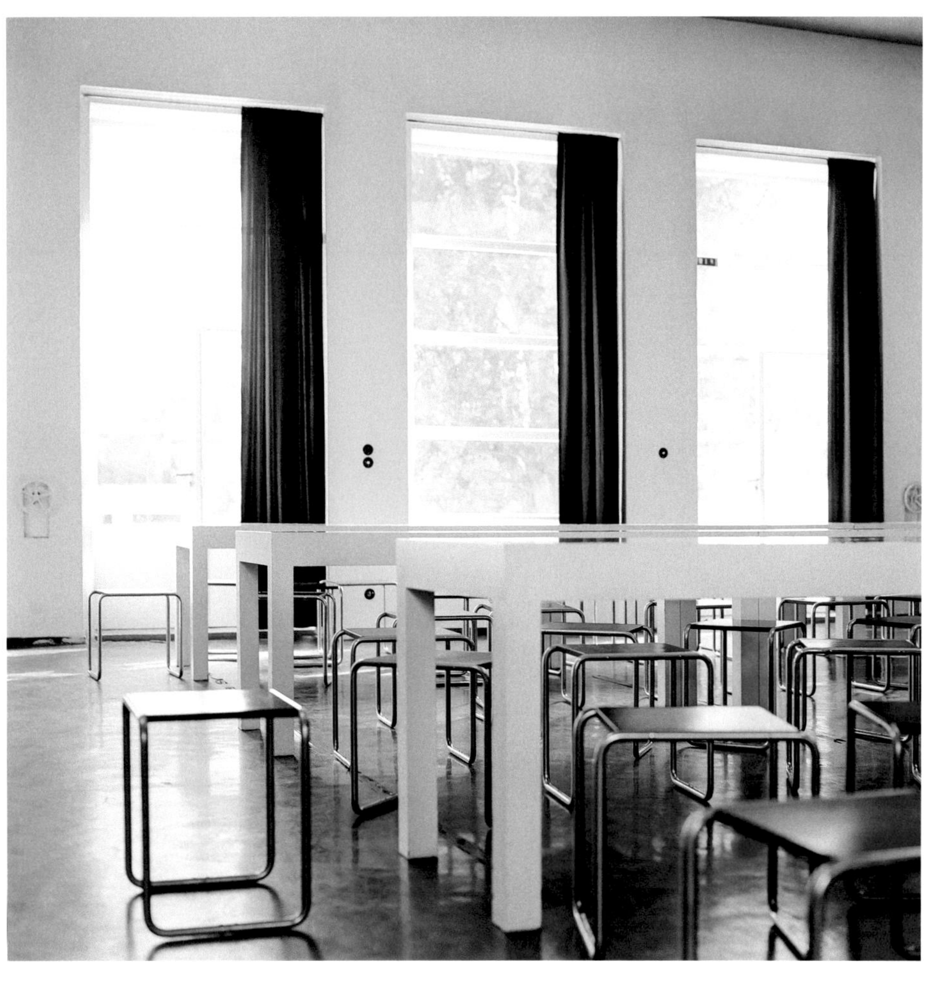

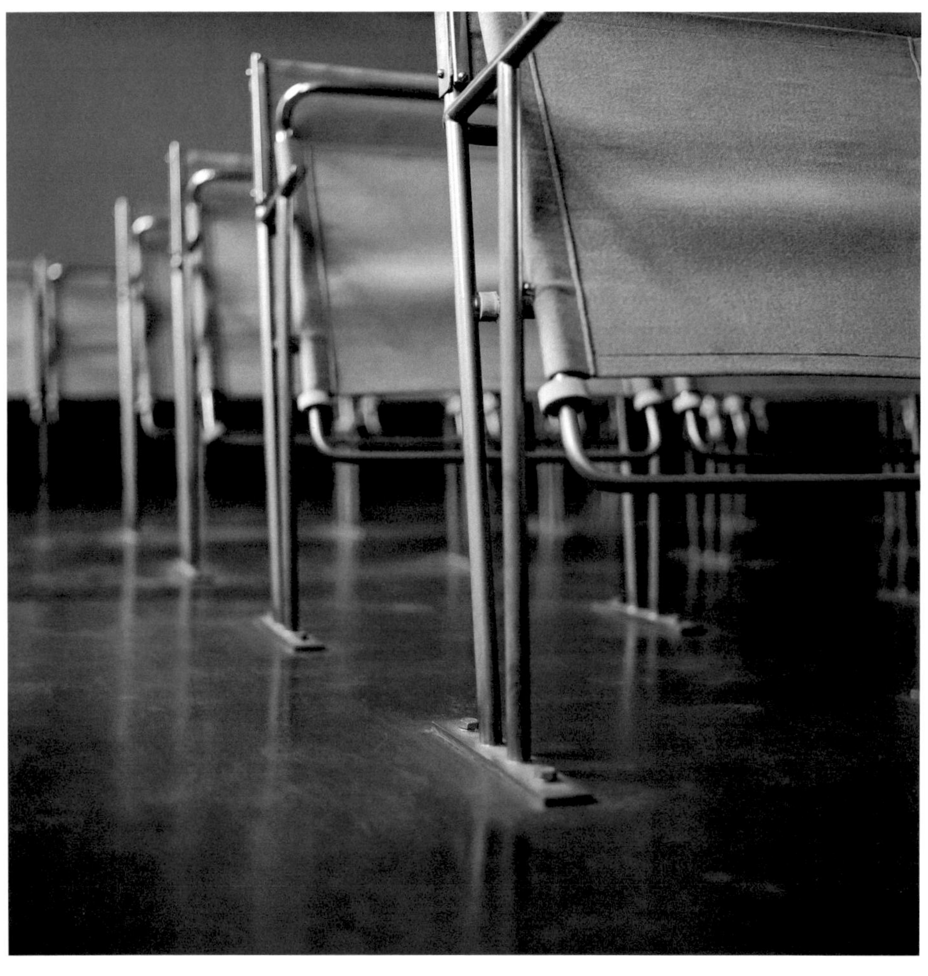

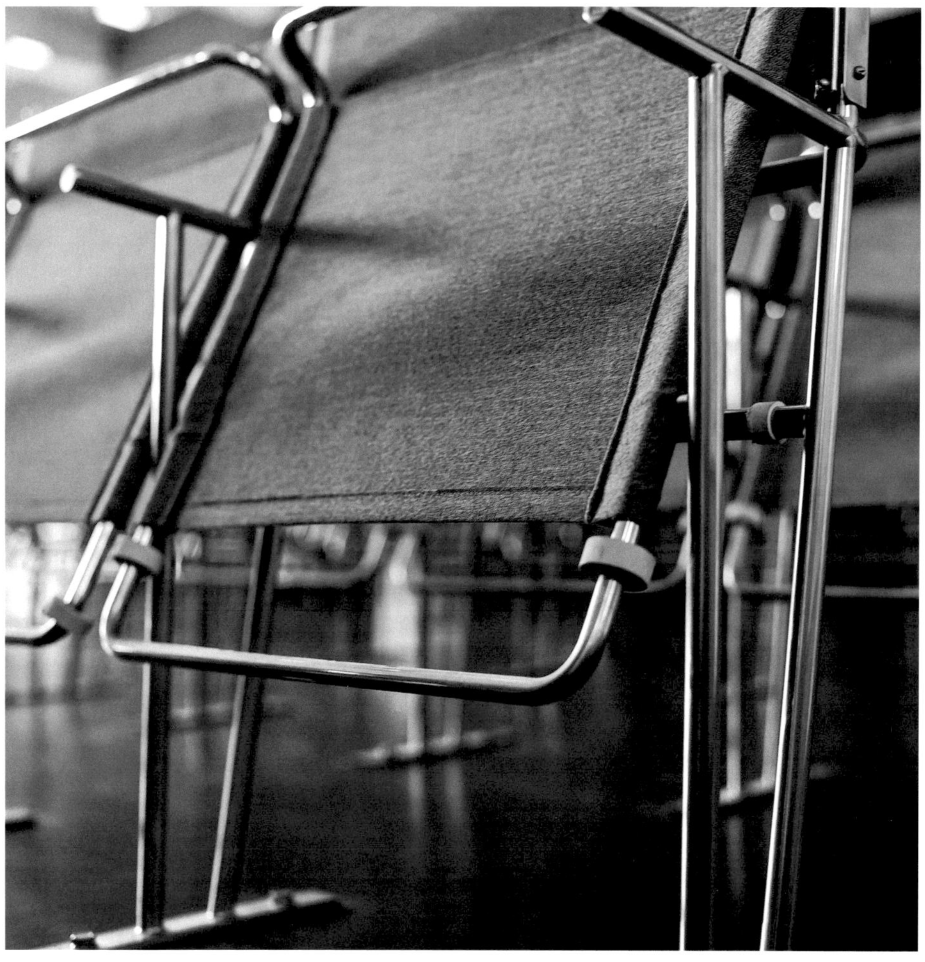

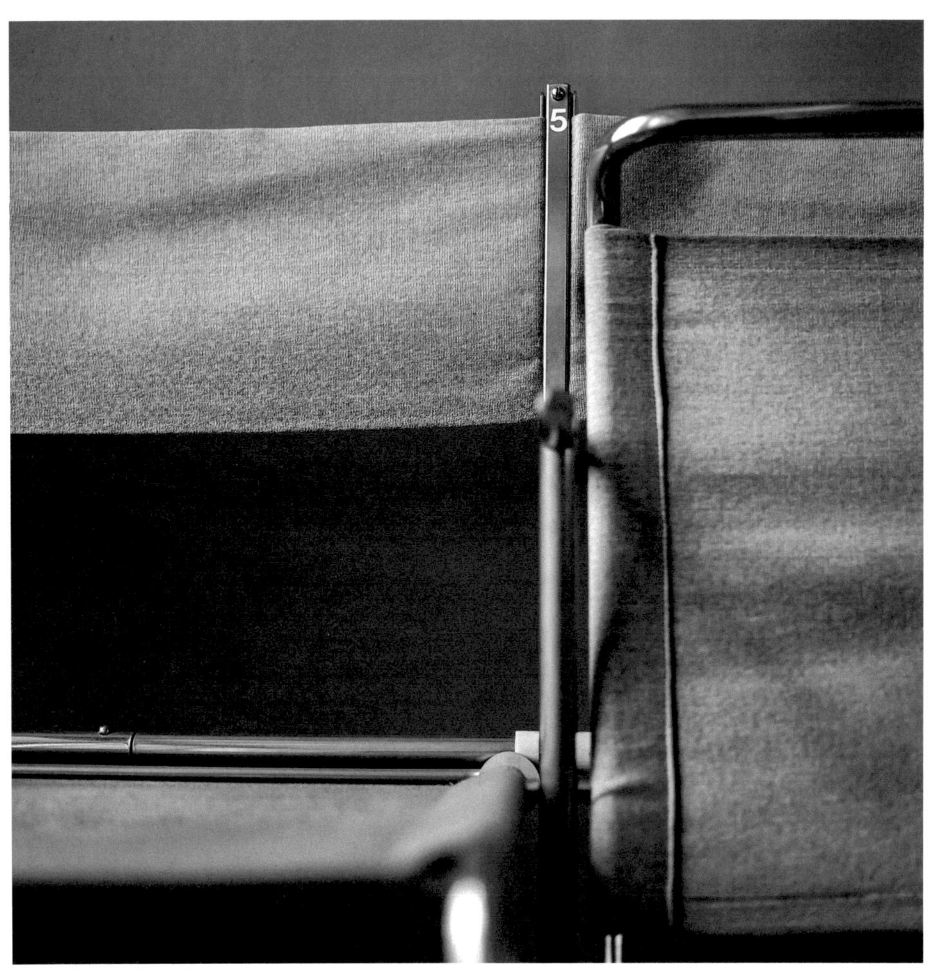

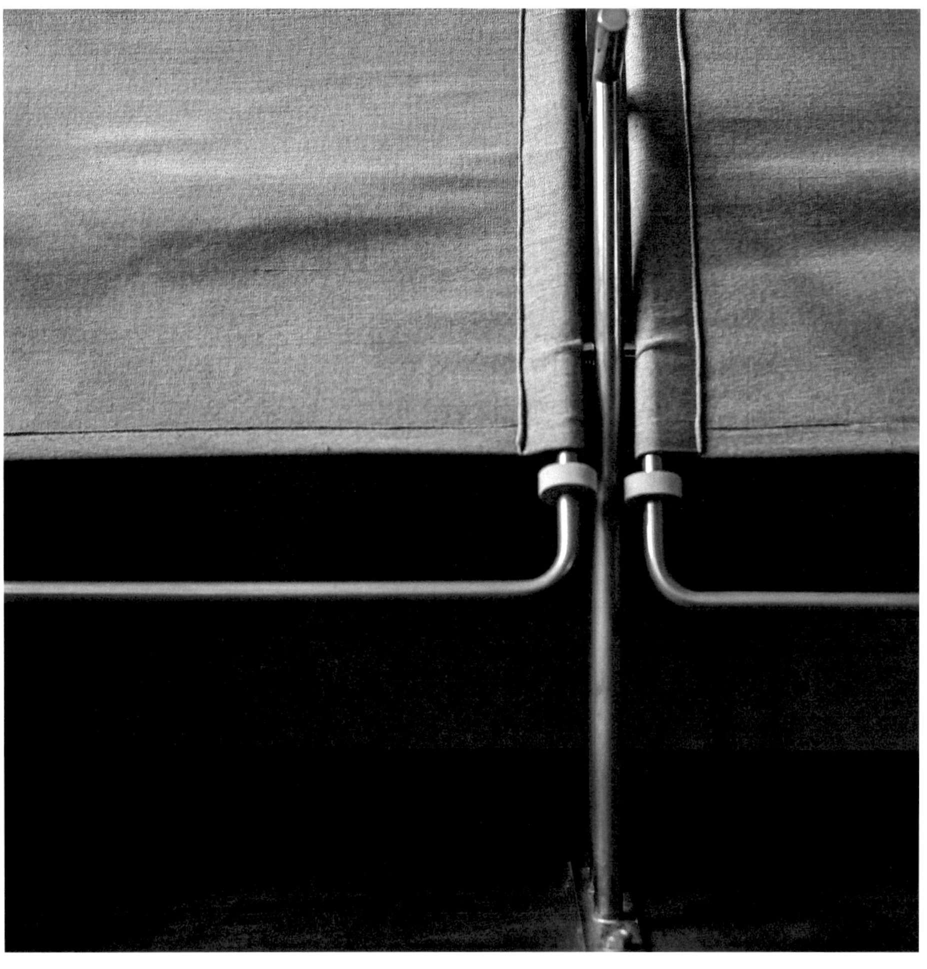

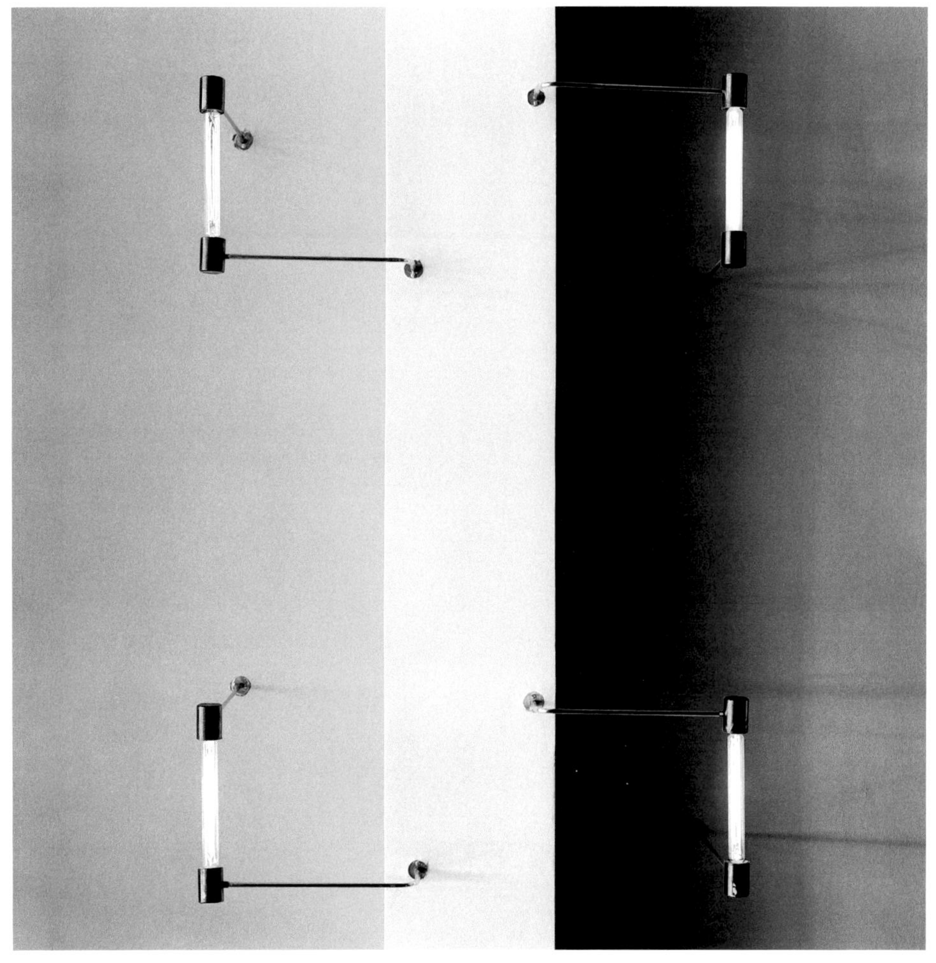

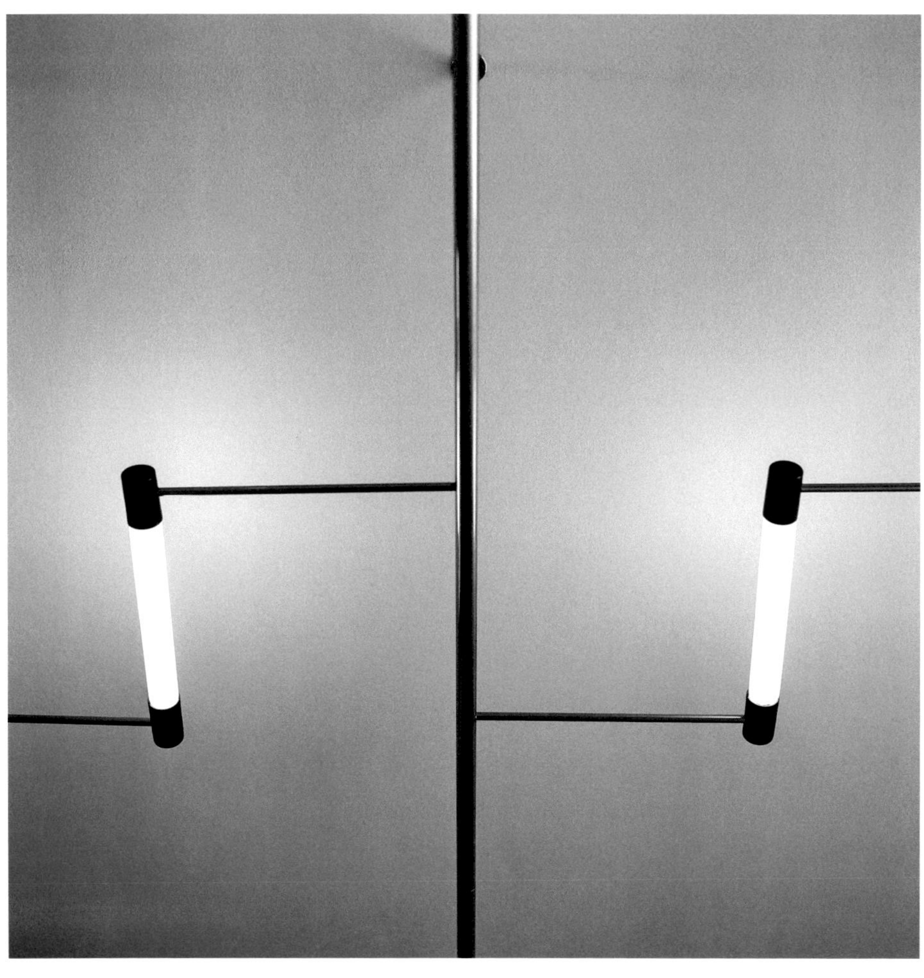

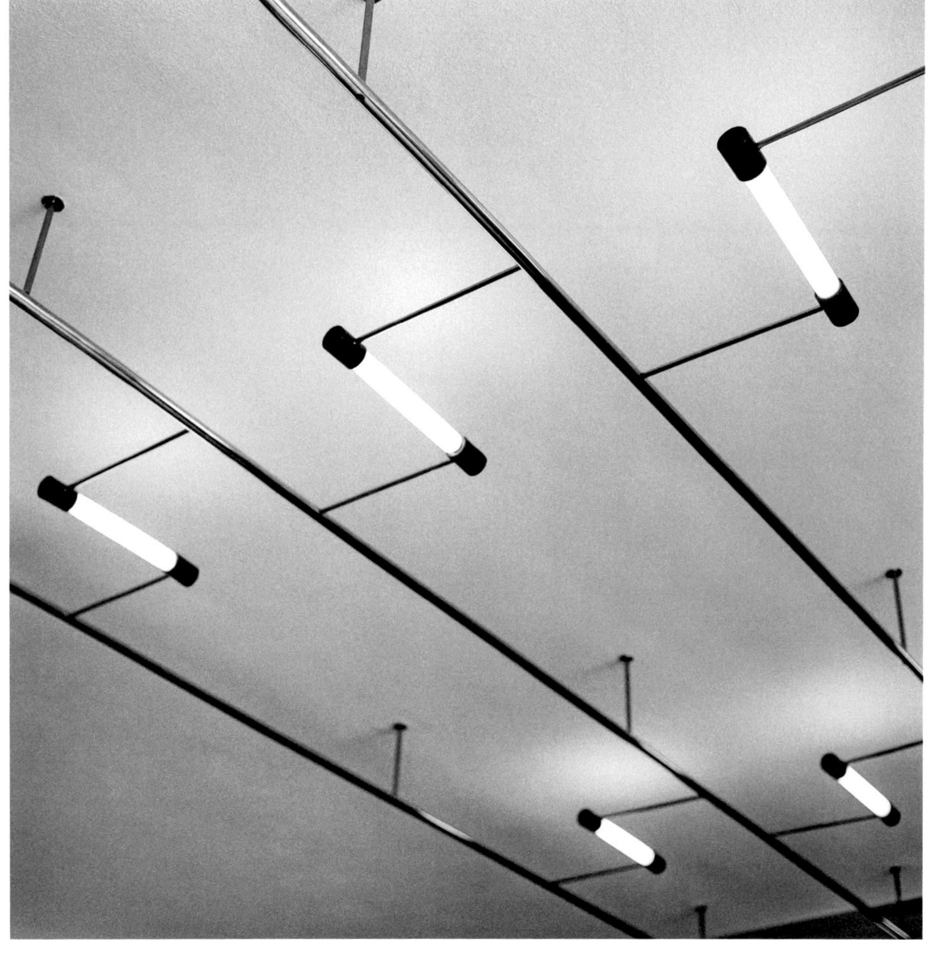

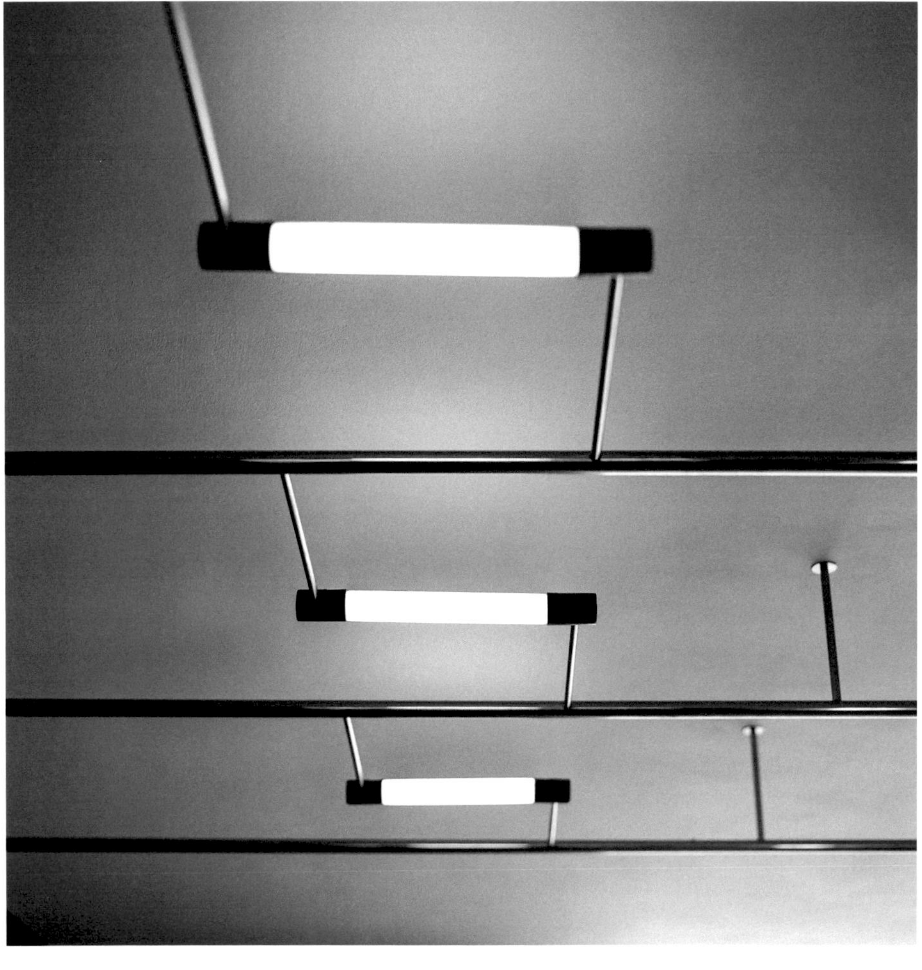

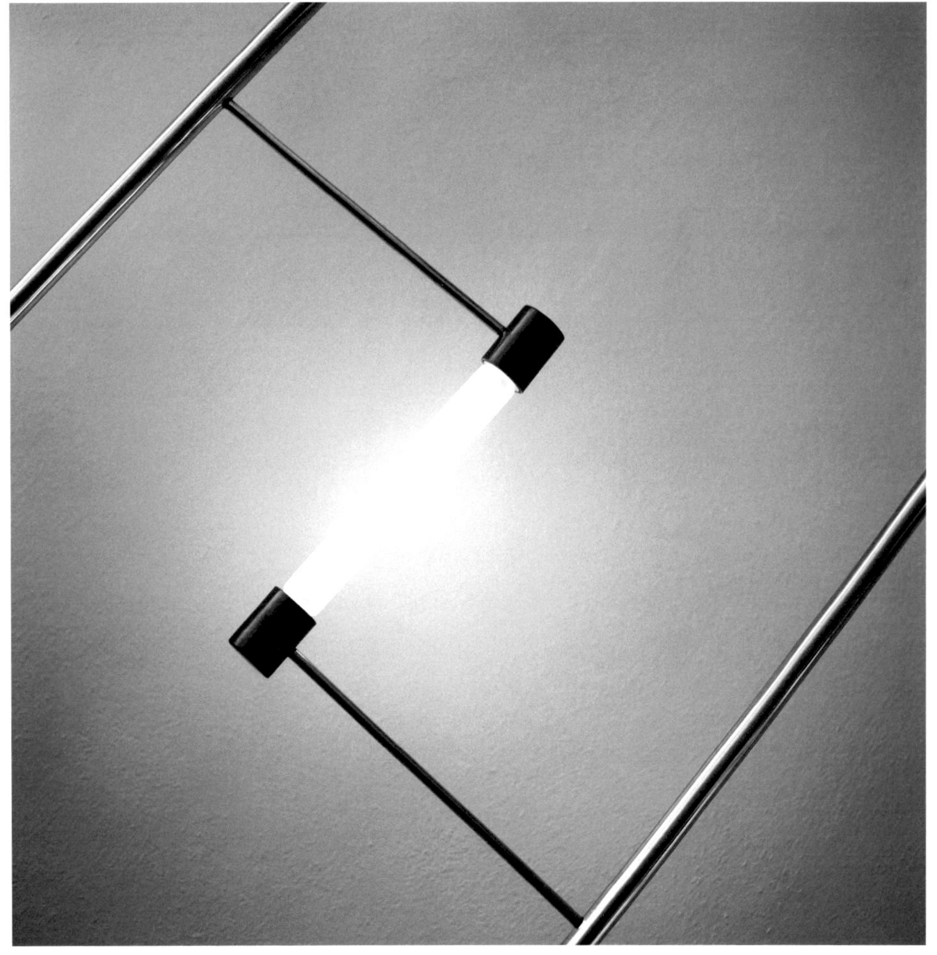

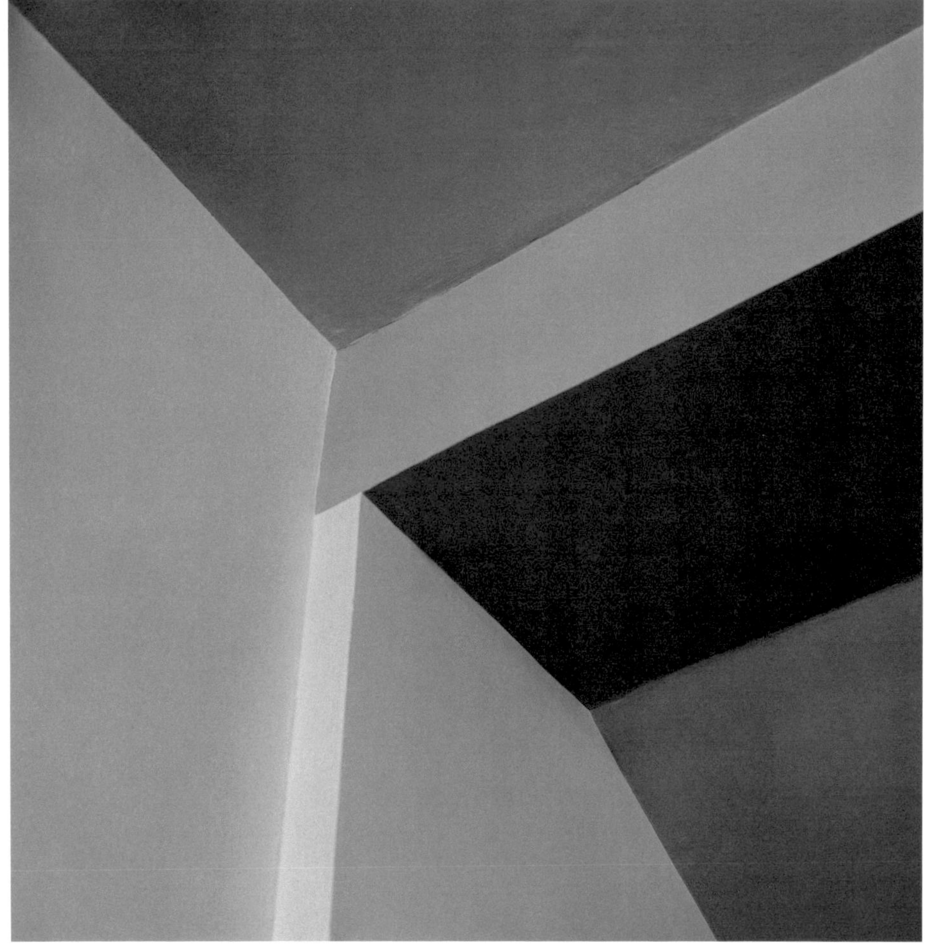

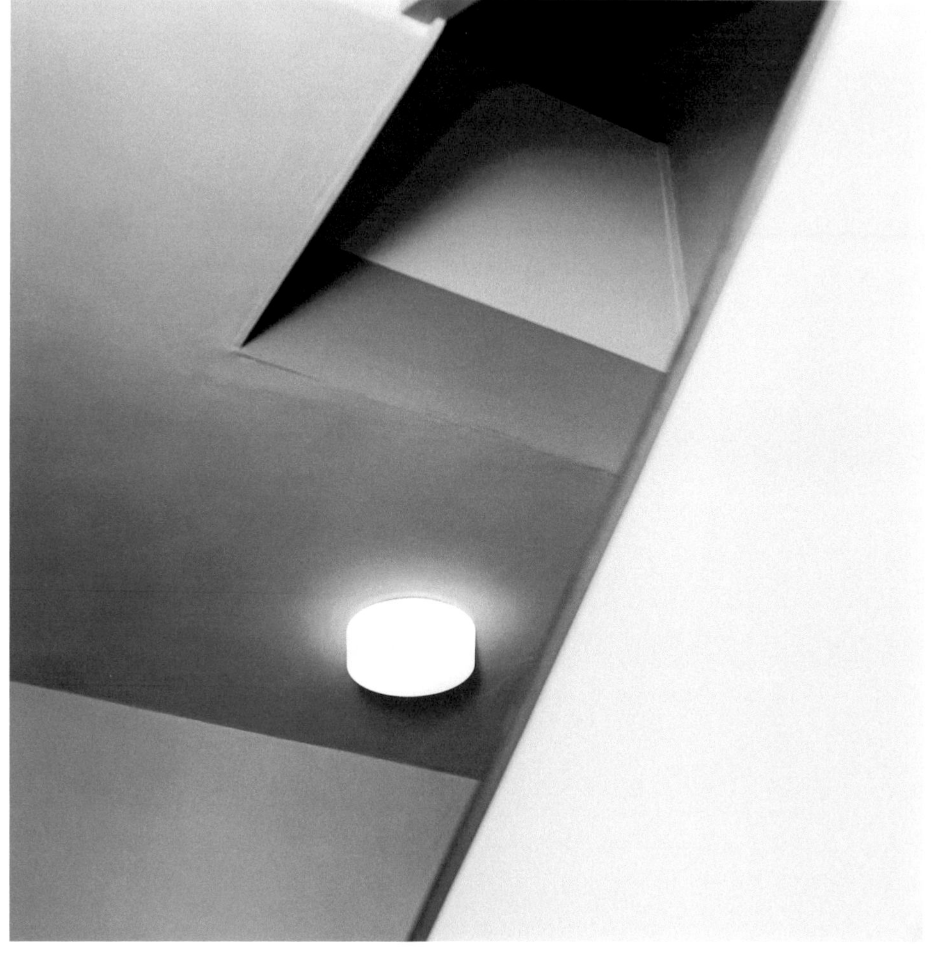

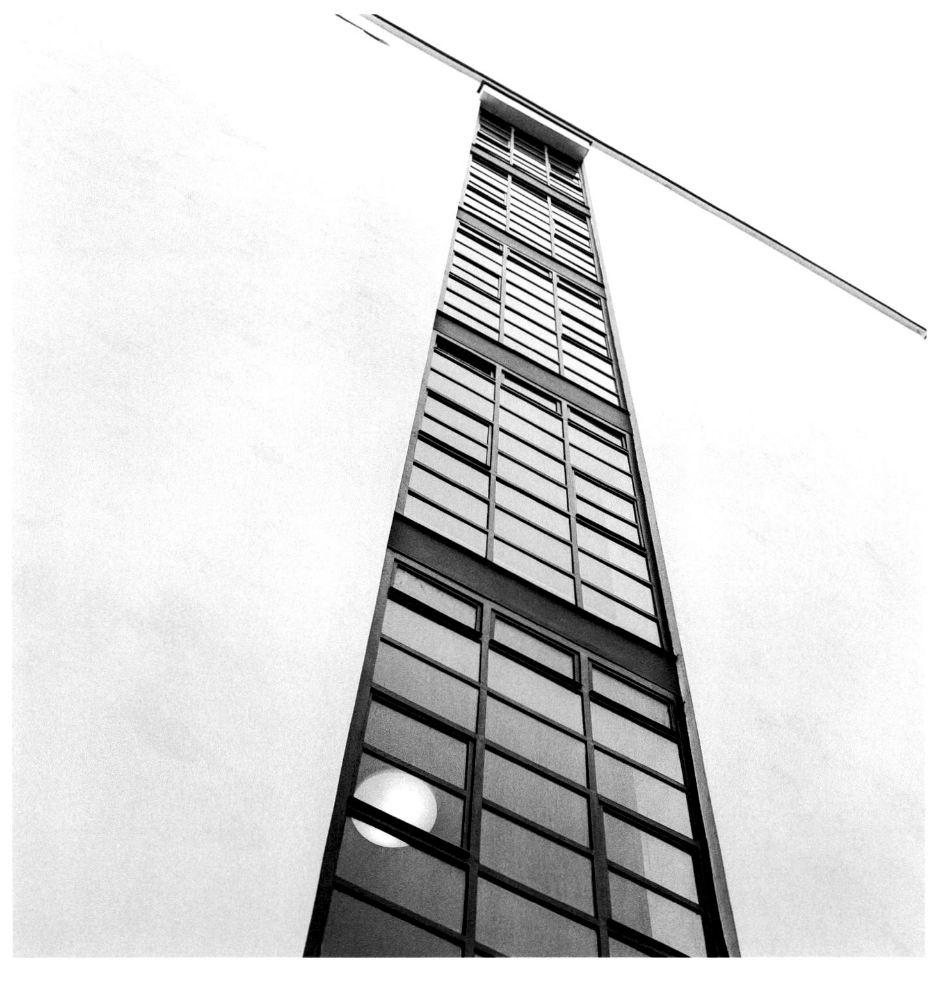

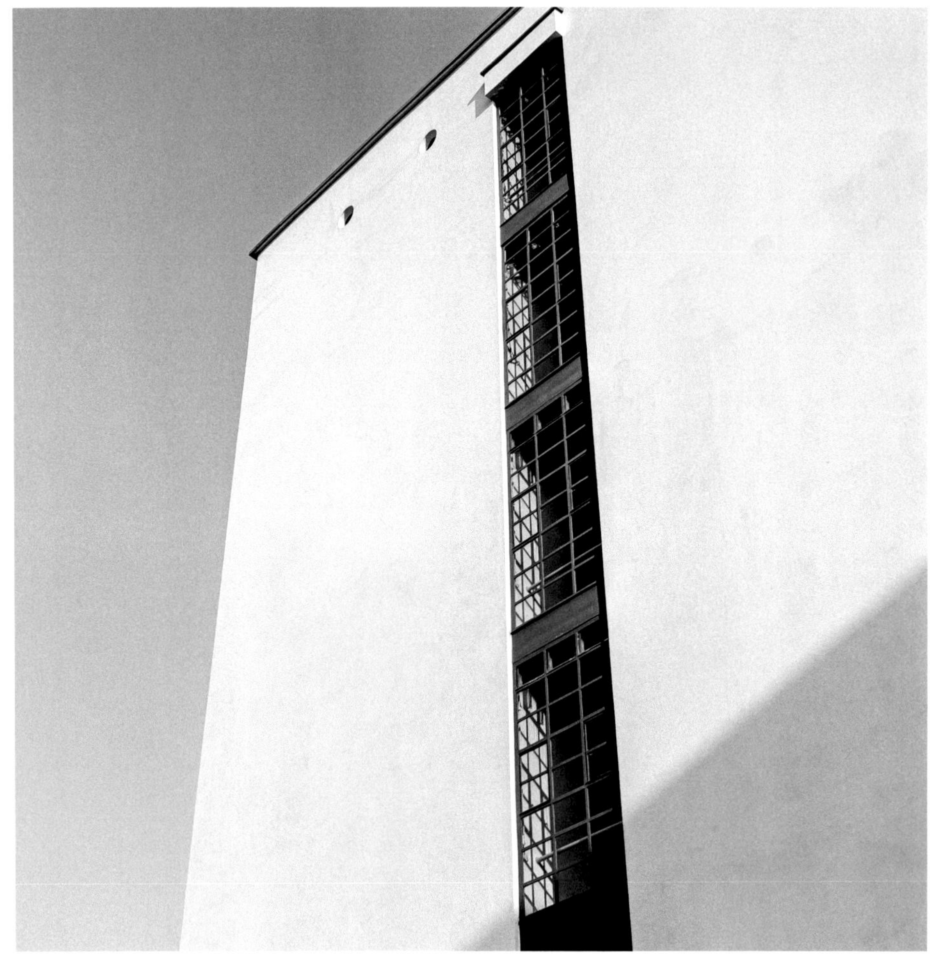

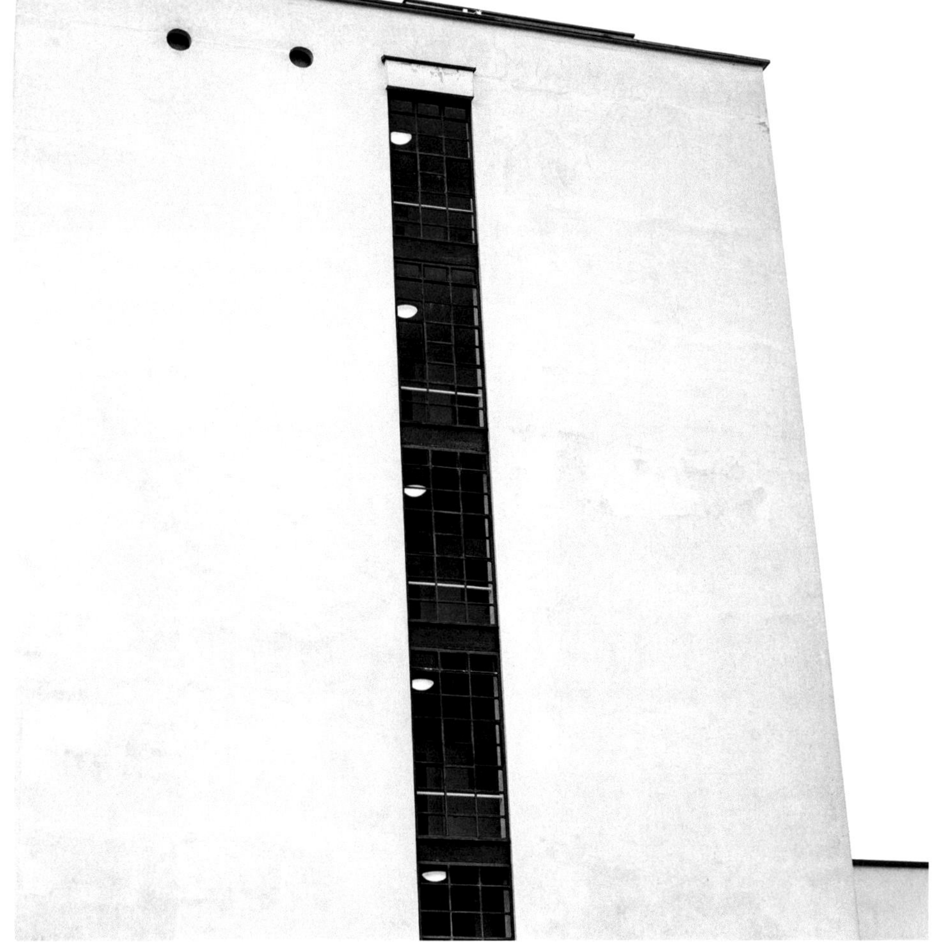

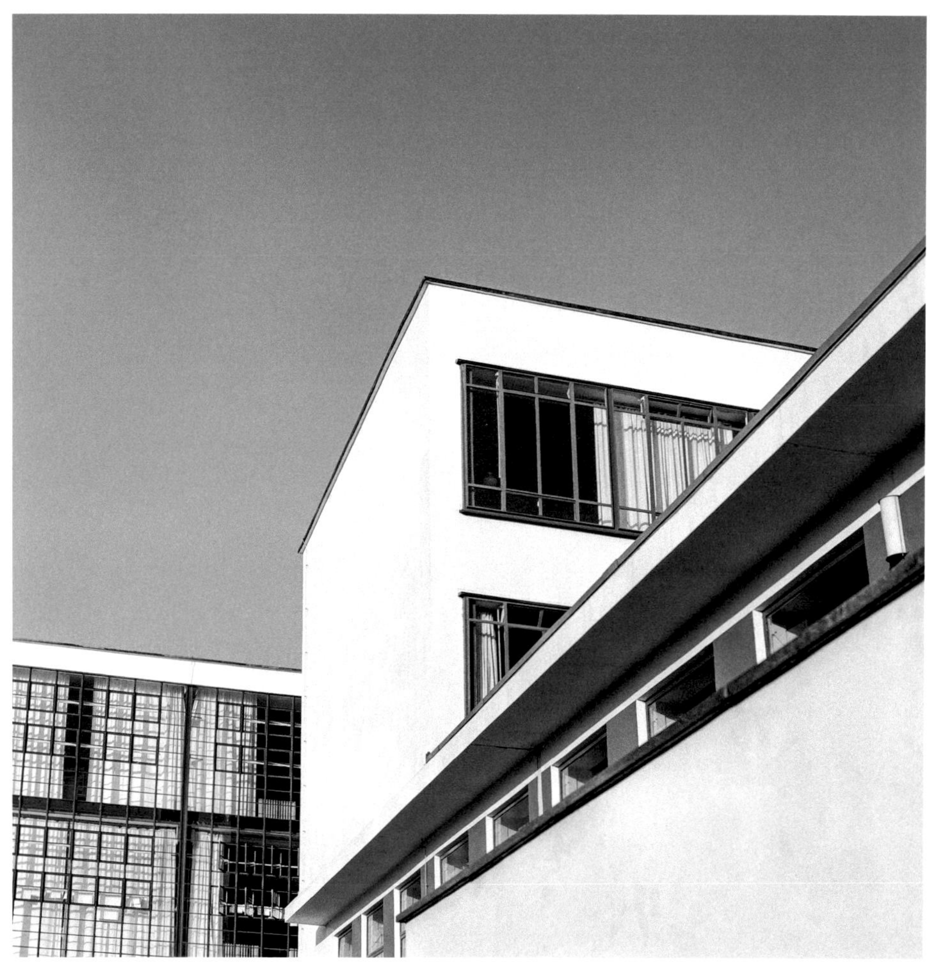

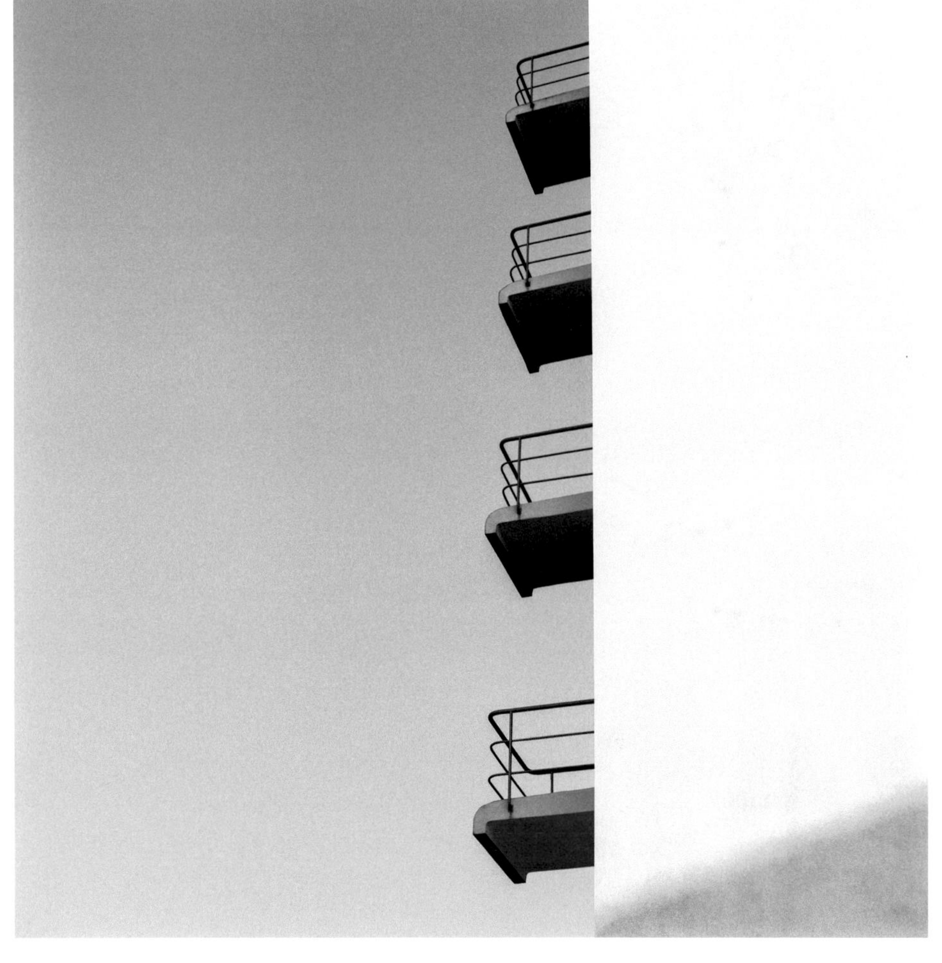

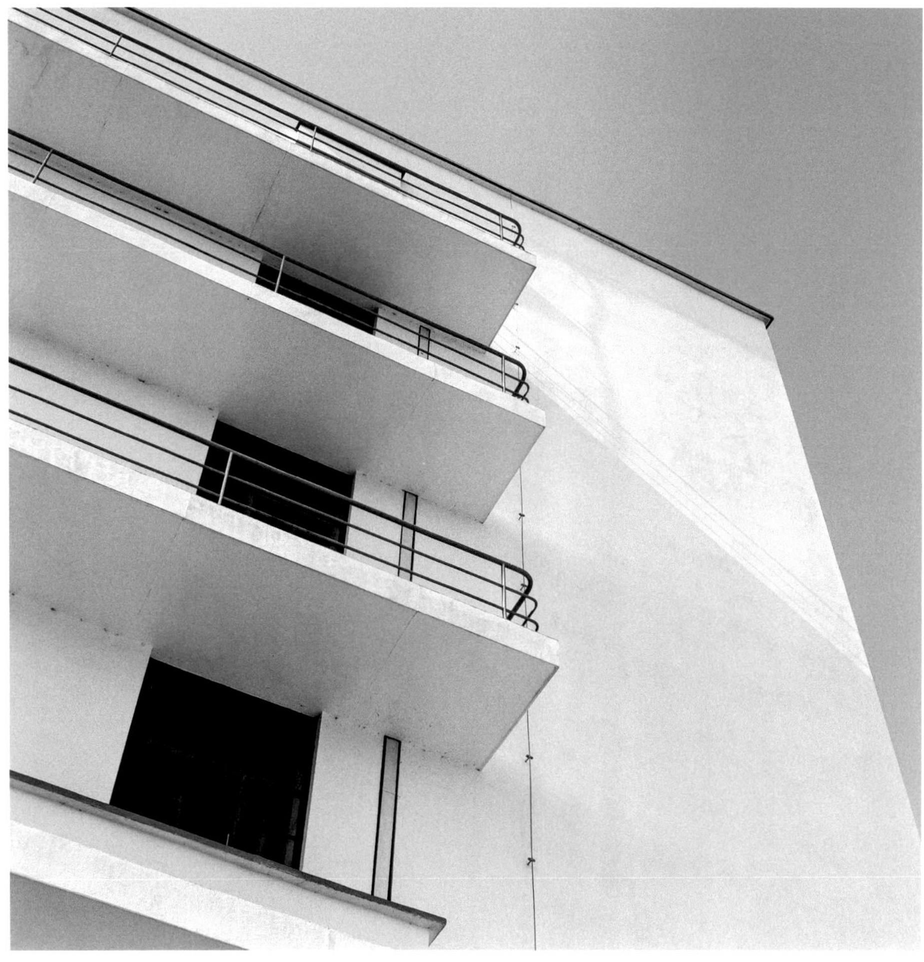

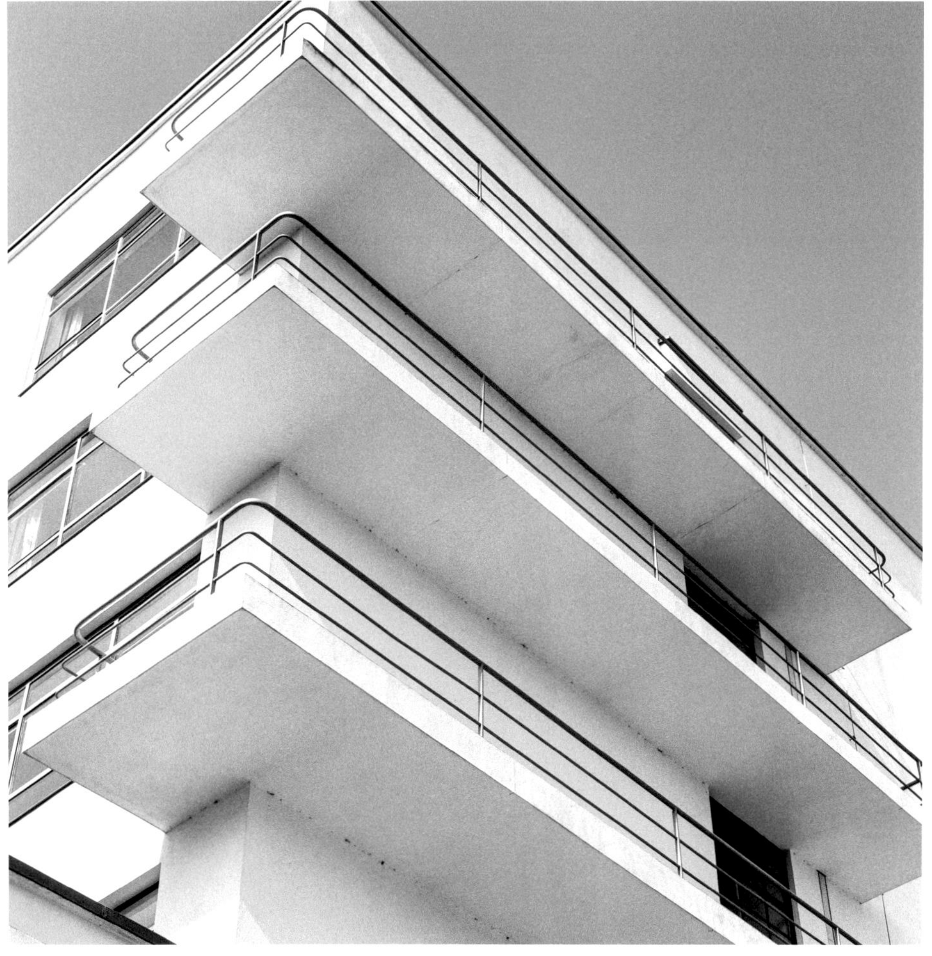

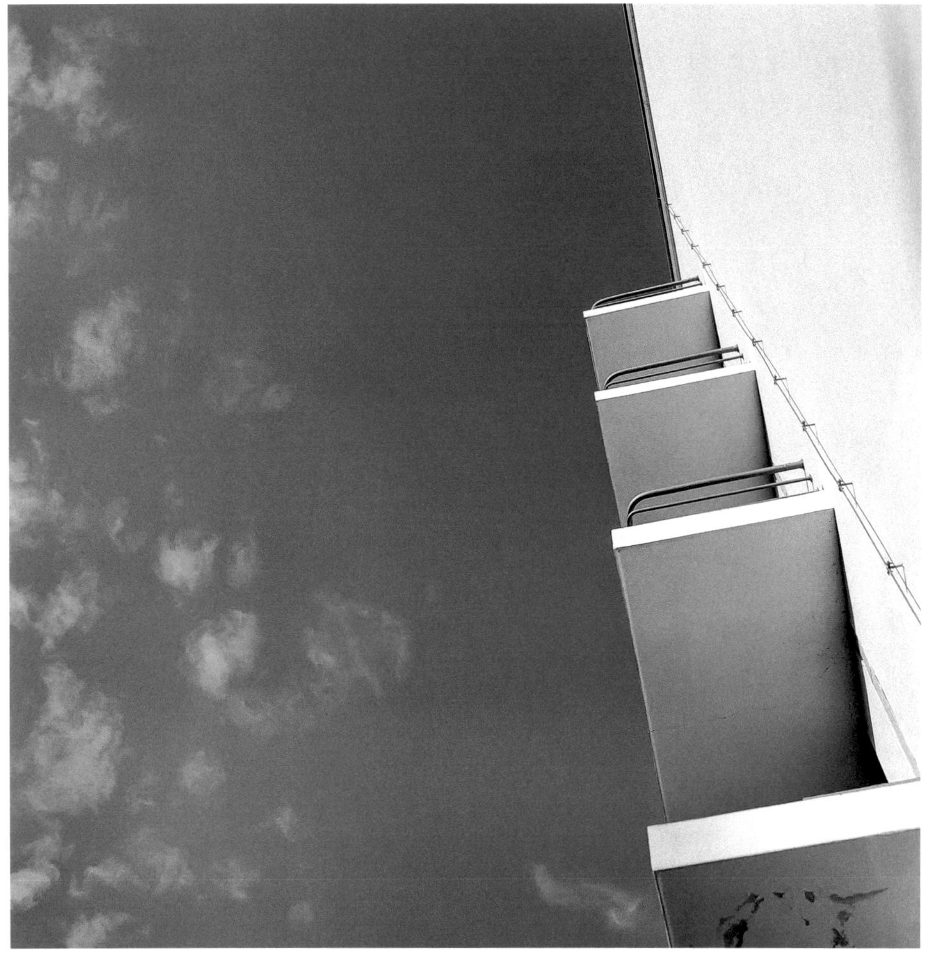

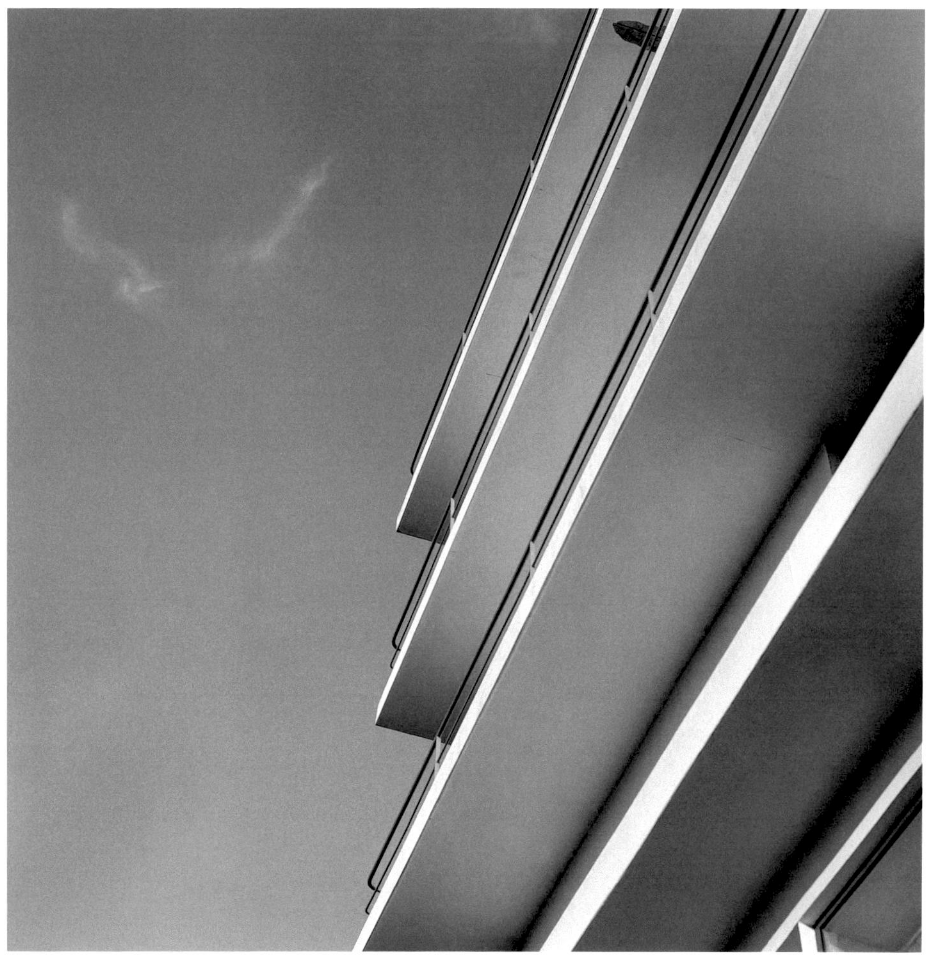

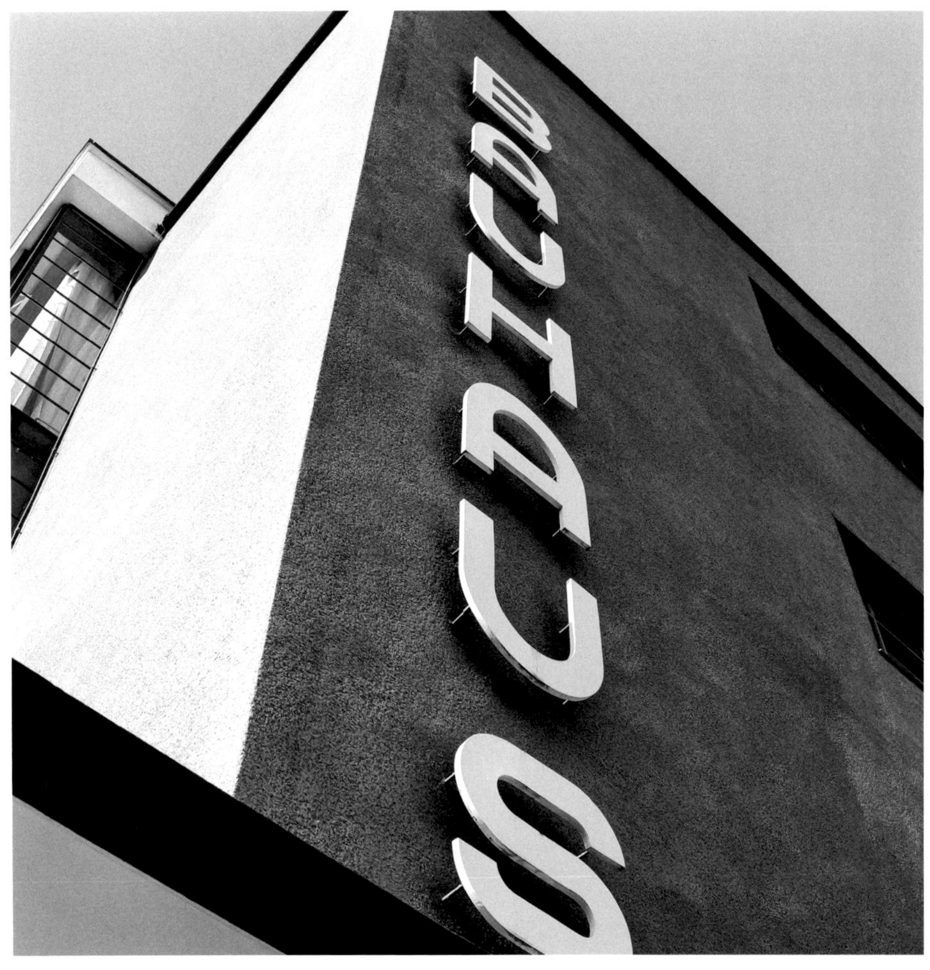
BAUHAUS

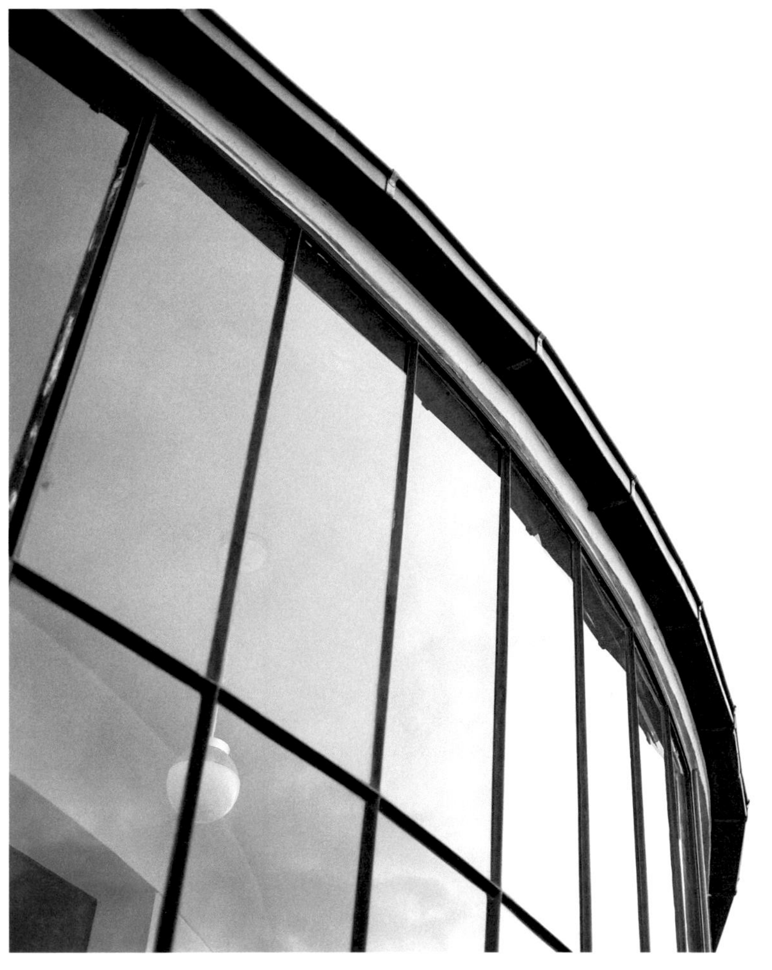

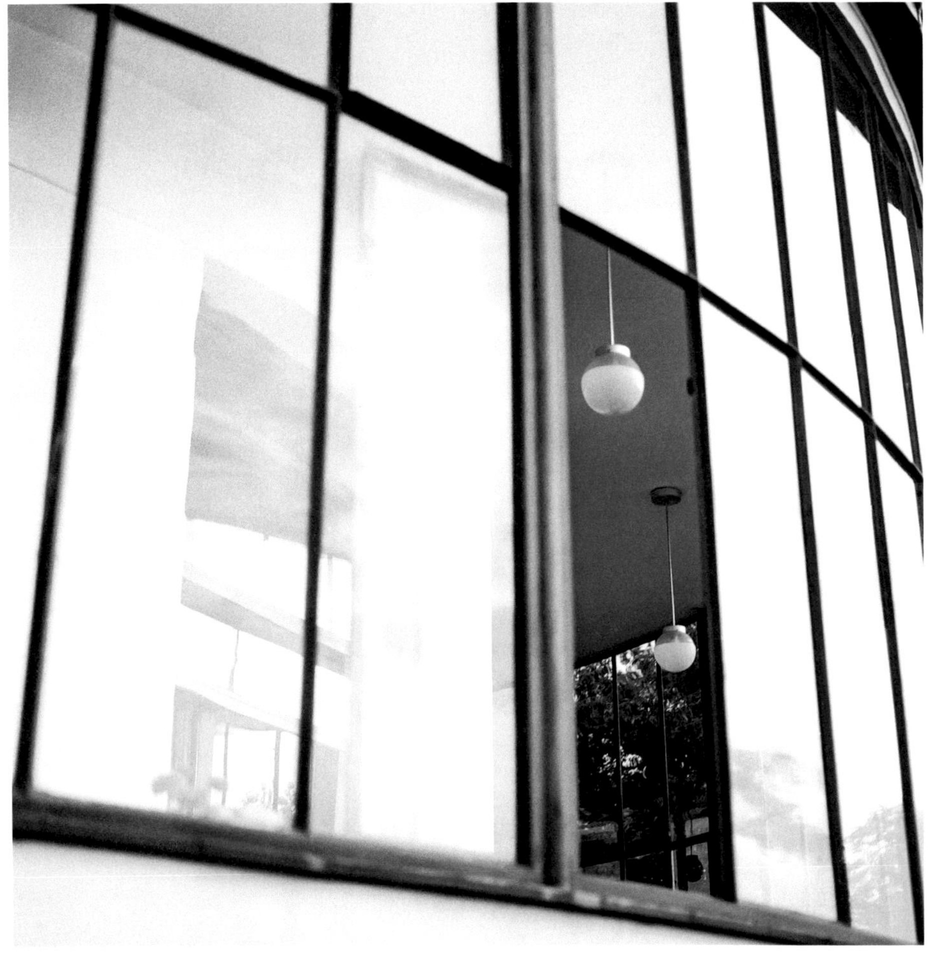

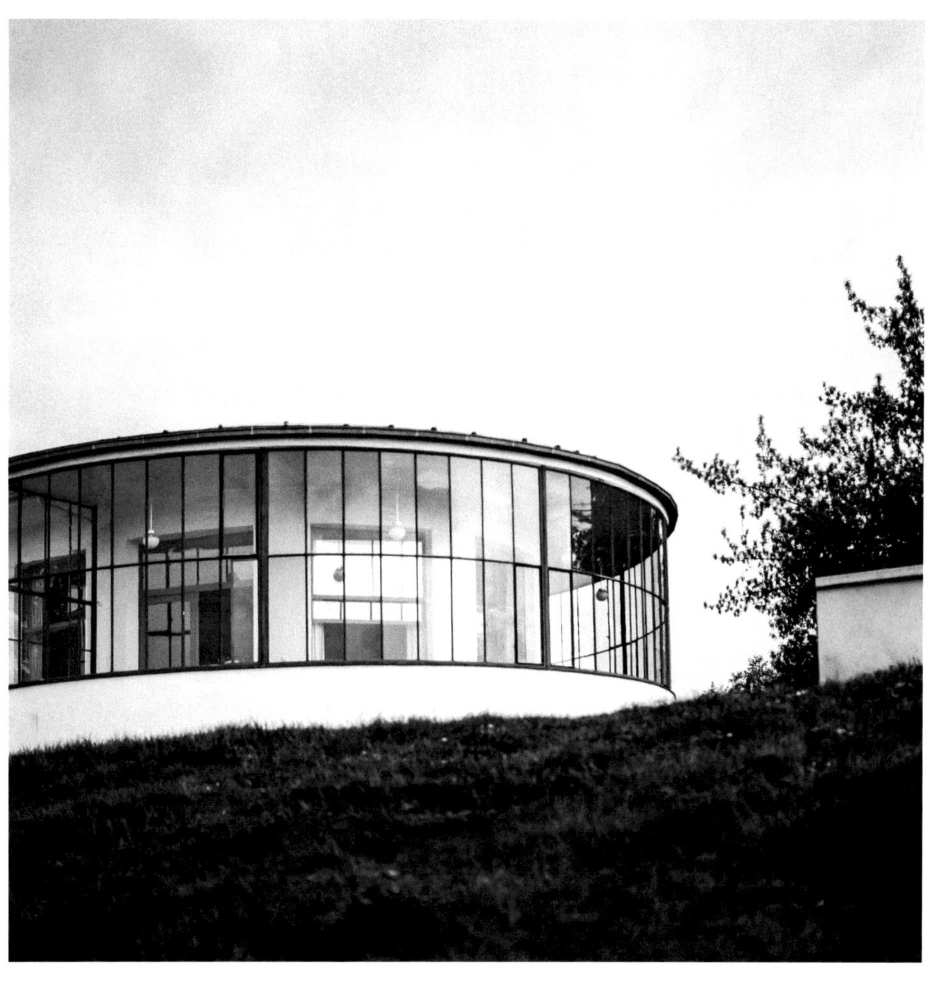

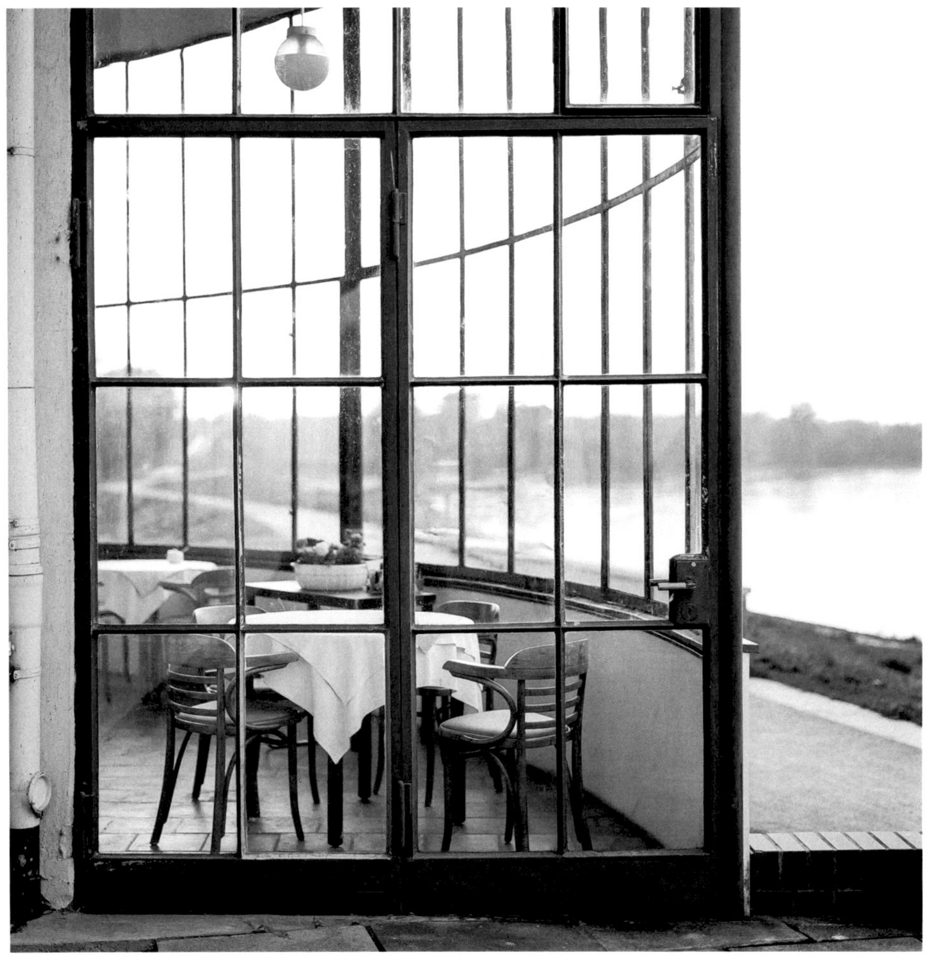

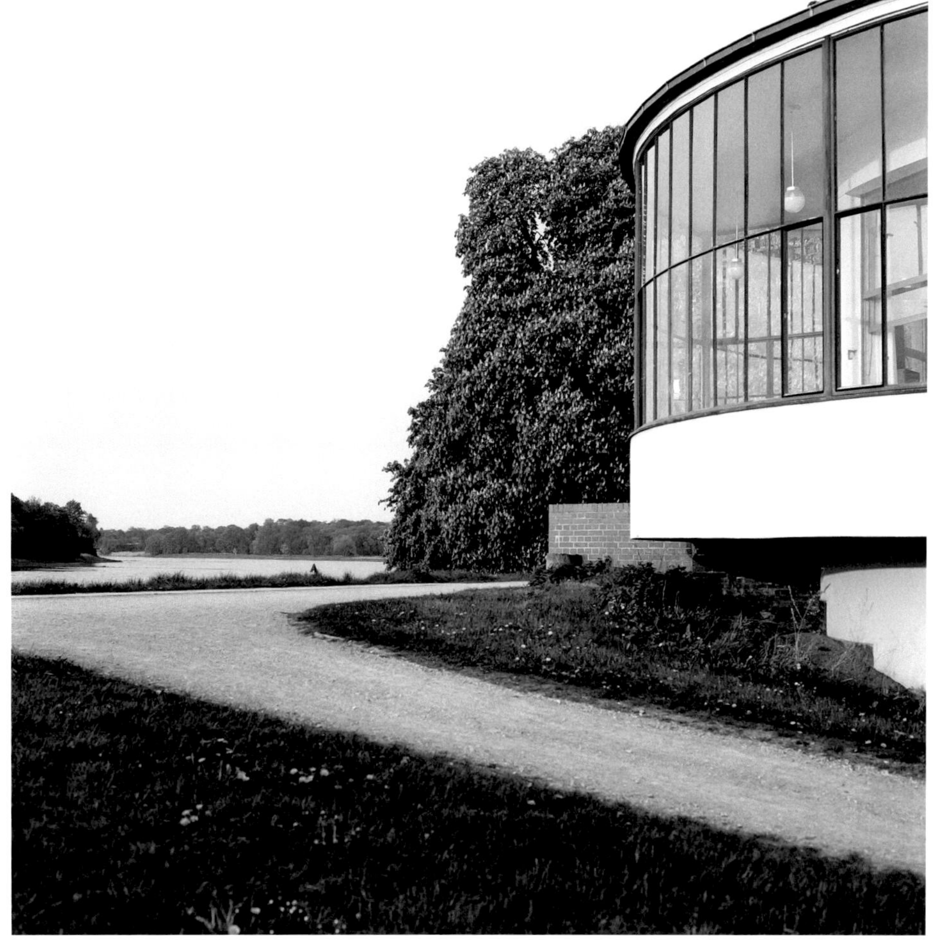

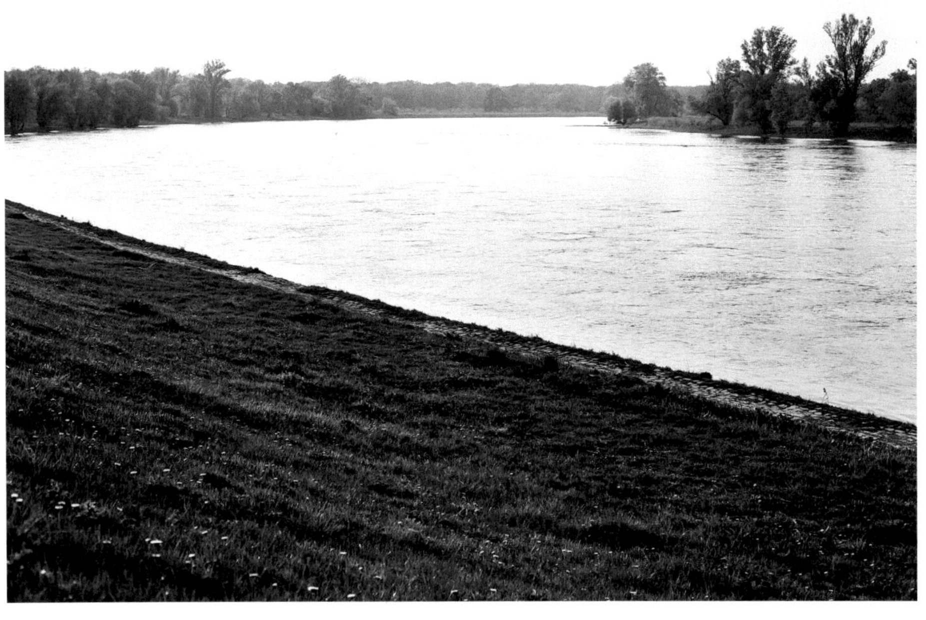

eine fotografische annäherung

EIN TEXT VON PROF. WIEBKE LOEPER

stefan berg kam 2008 als lehrbeauftragter für fotografie für drei semester zur vertretung an die hochschule anhalt nach dessau. bereits 2004 hatte er begonnen, am bauhaus zu fotografieren, angezogen von der anscheinend nie nachlassenden faszination dieser gestaltungsschule. nun selbst am ort des bauhauses fotografie vom grundkurs bis zum internationalen masterprogramm zu lehren, zwang ihn zu einer intensiven inhaltlichen beschäftigung über den mythos hinaus.

stefan bergs bilder zeugen von zwei ebenen der auseinandersetzung, einerseits mit der lehre, dem gedankensystem, und andererseits mit dem realen gebäude und dessen aura. „wie kann ich zeigen, was man nicht sieht?", ist eine der grundfragen in der lehre von lászló moholy-nagy. stefan berg beantwortet sie atmosphärisch, indem er durch und um die gebäude streift, treppauf treppab, hinaus um die ecken und hinunter bis zum kornhaus an die elbe. niemand begegnet ihm und die abwesenheit der großen meister scheint uns herauszufordern, uns selbst zu fragen, was eigentlich das faszinierende an den ideen des bauhauses ist. auf diese mentale reise nimmt stefan berg die hasselblad als begleiterin mit, ein hochentwickeltes mechanisches gerät, eine mittelformatkamera, mit der sich auch ohne stativ aus der hand fotografieren lässt. schaut man durch den lichtschacht der analogen kamera, dann muss das gehirn umdenken, da das bild gespiegelt ist und wir intuitiv die kamera genau in die andere richtung bewegen, um den gewünschten ausschnitt zu erhalten. das bild torkelt, und wir müssen uns auf einen tanz mit dem gerät einlassen. berg bleibt bei sich selbst und setzt bewusst auf entschleunigung. die feinheit des mechanischen handwerksgeräts symbolisiert für ihn beständigkeit und kontinuität. er arbeitet mit einer festbrennweite. das heißt, er muss sich bewegen, die kamera ist dabei starr und fordert entscheidungen. so hat sich berg auch gegen farbe entschieden – er reduziert das gesehene auf grauwerte und kontraste. aus seiner sicht würde farbe bei diesen bildern nur ablenken, die farbe wäre ein eigenes buch, so berg. die tonwerte zwischen schwarz und weiß deklinieren die fotografien, licht und schatten zaubern den raum am bauhaus. die fläche wird durch das licht strukturiert, der raum temporär konstruiert, das bild eingeschrieben ins negativ, schließlich auf papier gedruckt. in der zeit wandelt sich das bild ständig, die fotografie hält fest, schneidet aus und erst die dramaturgie des buches setzt die bilder wieder zu einem fluss zusammen.

berg spielt mit ähnlichkeit und wiederholung, mit dem leicht versetzten blick, und erzählt auf diese weise geschichten über den raum. das gemeinsame der aufeinanderfolgenden bilder steigert die intensität des erlebens. berg nutzt oft das nach-oben-schauen, einen blickwinkel, den wir von rodtschenko kennen. sein blickwinkel ist nicht extrem, vielmehr verweist er uns auf die begehung des ortes und spürt den zeichen nach, die uns durch die zeugenschaft der architektur und gestaltung der dinge viel über die geistige haltung am bauhaus verraten – seien es die umlenkrollen, stuhlbeine, lichtschalter oder türgriffe. die bilder erzählen von der betonung des materials, des technischen, des funktionalen, von proportionen und bezügen.

gelingt es berg mit seinen reduzierten, klaren bildern, den glauben an eine welt, die nach klaren prinzipien organisiert ist, an eine unverrückbare ordnung, sichtbar zu machen? spüren wir die utopie in der aura des gebäudes? ist es ein romantischer blick, mit dem uns berg führt? vielleicht, doch er wirft uns auf uns selbst zurück, als würden wir durch die räume streifen und uns selbst vergewissern, ob die faszination des bauhauses noch auf uns wirkt oder wo wir vielleicht gegen sie rebellieren.

a photographic approach

A TEXT BY WIEBKE LOEPER

stefan berg came to anhalt university of applied sciences in dessau in 2008 as an appointed lecturer in photography for three semesters. earlier in 2004 he had begun photographing the bauhaus, attracted by a seemingly unwavering fascination with the design school. teaching photography at the bauhaus, from foundation courses up to the international master program, drew him into an intensive, substantive engage-ment above and beyond the myth.

stefan berg´s photographs evidence two levels of confrontation, on the one hand with teaching, the system of thought, and on the other hand with the real existing building and its aura. "how can i show what one does not see?" is one of the basic questions in the teaching of lászló moholy-nagy. stefan berg answers it atmospherically, wandering through and around the buildings, up and down the stairs, around the corners and down to the kornhaus next to the elbe. nobody encounters him, and the absence of the great masters appears to challenge us to ask ourselves what it is that really fascinates us about the ideas of the bauhaus. on this mental journey, stefan berg takes the hasselblad as his companion, a sophisticated mechanical device, a medium format camera, with which photography can also be taken handheld without a tripod. when looking through the light shaft of the analog camera, the brain has to think differently, because the image is mirrored. we intuitively move the camera in the wrong direction while trying to obtain the desired framing. the image torques, and we have to engage in a dance with the device.
berg abides by himself and consciously pursues a slowing down. for him, the fineness of the mechanical, handcrafted device symbolizes stability and continuity. he works with a fixed focal length. that means he has to move around, the camera remaining rigid and demanding his deceleration. berg also decided against color – he reduces the visible to gray tones and contrasts.

from his point of view, color would only cause a distraction from these photographs. color would be its own book, according to berg. the tonal values between black and white inflect the photographs. light and shadow conjure up the space of the bauhaus. the surface is structured through light, the space temporarily constructed, the image inscribed on the negative then finally printed on paper. throughout time, the image continuously changes. photography arrests it, cuts it out of time. only the dramaturgy of the book rejoins the images into one and the same flow.

berg plays with similarity and repetition, with the slightly shifted view, and in this way he tells stories about the space. the commonalities among the consecutive photographs boost the intensity of their experience.
berg often uses the 'looking-above', a viewing angle we know from rodchenko. his viewpoint is not extreme. rather, it references the act of walking around the place. it traces the signs that, through the testimony of the architecture and general shape of things, reveal a great deal to us about the residual mindset at the bauhaus – whether they be pulleys, chair legs, light switches or door handles. the photographs tell us about the emphasis of the material, the technical, the functional, about proportions and relations.

with his reduced, clear photographs, does berg succeed in making visible the belief in a world organized according to clear principles, an unshakeable order? do we sense this utopia in the aura of the building? is it a romantic gaze with which berg guides us? maybe, but it returns our gaze upon ourselves again, as if we were wandering through the spaces and ascertaining whether the fascination of the bauhaus still affects us, or where we might rebel against it.

bildverzeichnis image index

MIT ANMERKUNGEN VON WITH COMMENTS BY STEFAN BERG

sämtliche fotografien stammen aus den jahren 2004–2009. die bilder wurden mit einer mechanischen hasselblad mittelformatkamera und einer normalbrennweite von zeiss auf agfa-film aufgenommen.
all pictures were taken between 2004 and 2009 with a mechanical hasselblad medium format camera on agfa-film with a zeiss standard focal length lens.

das in den fotografien dargestellte bauhausgebäude wurde in den jahren 1925/26 vom gründer des bauhauses walter gropius entworfen.
the bauhaus building that is illustrated in the photographs has been designed by the bauhaus founder walter gropius in 1925/26.

titel treppenhaus am haupteingang, brüstung und handlauf > die ansicht erinnert an das gemälde ‚bauhaustreppe' von oskar schlemmer main entrance staircase, balustrade and handrail > the view is reminiscent of the picture 'bauhaustreppe' by oskar schlemmer

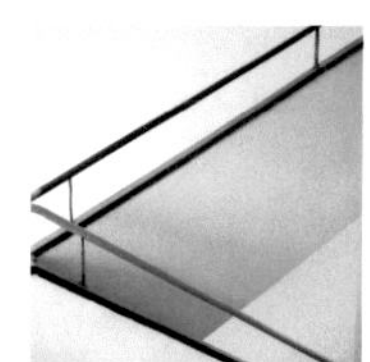

4 vestibül, untergeschoss, lichtknopf und steckdose aus bakelit vestibule, basement floor, light switch und socket made from bakelite

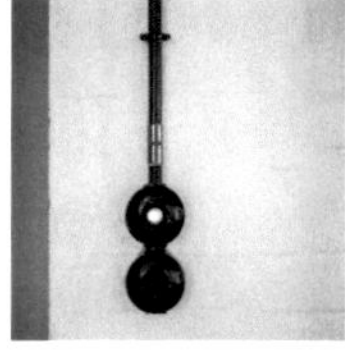

7 treppenhaus am haupteingang, treppenabsatz zum zweiten stock, heizung und pendelleuchte (entwurf marianne brandt, nachbau) > gropius ließ die junkers-heizkörper als symbol des technischen fortschritts an prominenter stelle aufhängen. früher hingen in repräsentativen bauten an dieser stelle familienportraits main en-trance staircase, landing leading to the second floor, radiator and pendant lamp (design marianne brandt, replical) > gropius had junkers-radiators installed in prominent places as a symbol of technical progress. in former times, in prestigious buildings, family portraits were hung here

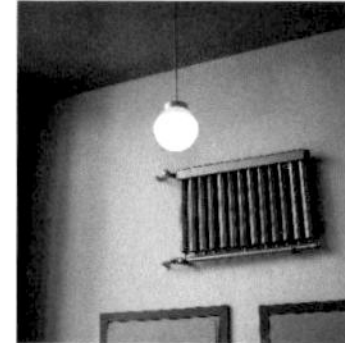

11 werkstattflügel, südseite, fassade mit bauhaus schriftzug (in anlehnung an einen schriftentwurf von herbert bayer) workshop wing, southside, facade with bauhaus lettering (following a type design by herbert bayer)

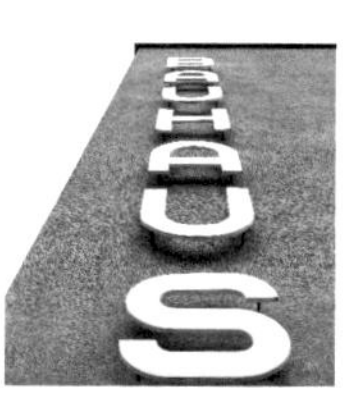

12 | 13 werkstattflügel, nordfassade, selbsttragende stahl-glas-konstruktion | westfassade mit südlichem eingang > durch den geringfügigen überhang und die weißen streifen am unteren ende wirkt das gebäude geradezu leicht. im dessau der vorkriegszeit gab es noch oft nebel, das gebäude schien dann zu schweben workshop wing, north facade, self-supporting glass and steel construction | west facade with south entrance > the building appears light because of the slight overhang and the white bottom rim of the facade. in prewar dessau there was often fog, so the building seemed to float

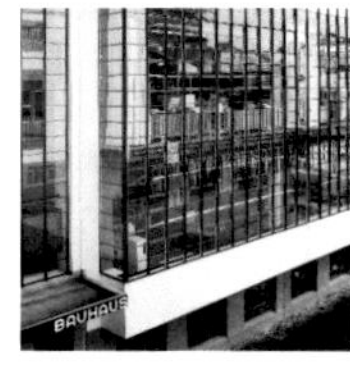

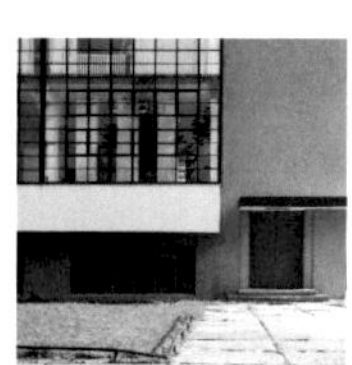

14 | 15 werkstattflügel, nordfassade, sockel und selbsttragende stahl-glas-konstruktion | unter der brücke, blick auf den haupteingang > das rechte foto spiegelt meiner meinung nach die absicht von walter gropius wieder, hochhäuser zu konstruieren – die fassade scheint unbegrenzt verlängerbar

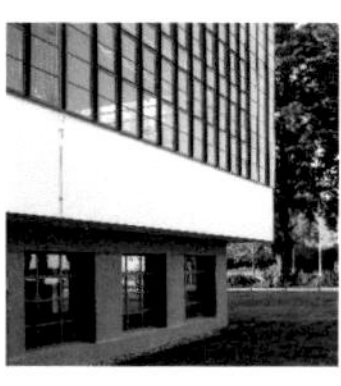

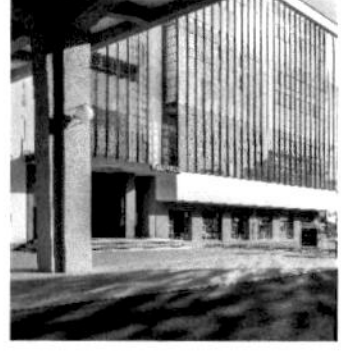

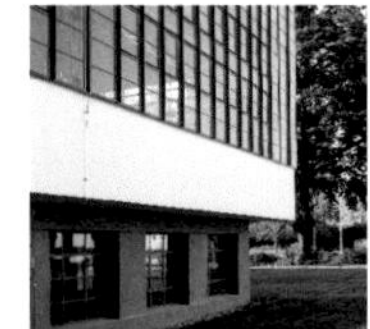
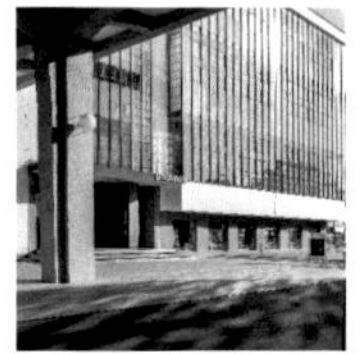

14 | 15 workshop wing, north facade, base and self-supporting glass and steel construction | underneath the bridge, view to the north facade > in my opinion the picture on the right hand side mirrors the aim of walter gropius to construct skyscrapers – the facade gives the impression to go on infinetly

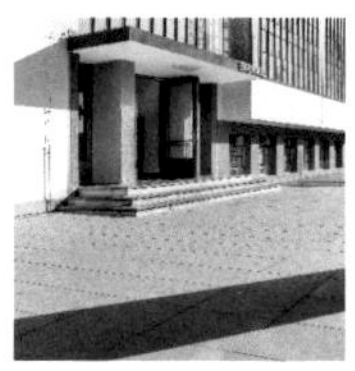

17 haupteingang, blick von der bauhausstraße > es war faszinierend, schon vor dem gebäude ein zusammenspiel hoher lichtkontraste mit essenziellen gestaltungs- und erscheinungsformen zu entdecken. ob das so geplant war? main entrance, view from the bauhausstraße > it was fascinating to already find an interplay between extreme light contrasts, basic design elements and outward forms around the main entrance. was that intentionally planned?

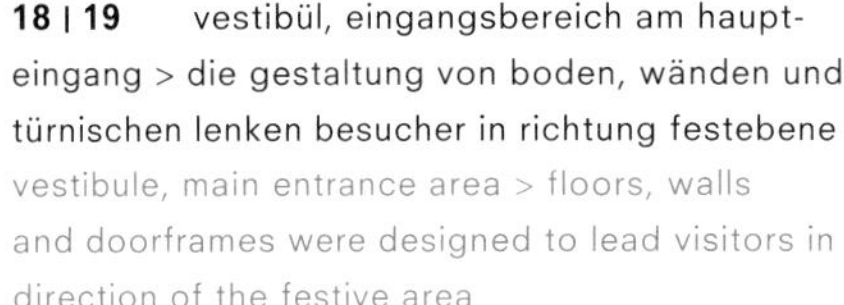

18 | 19 vestibül, eingangsbereich am haupteingang > die gestaltung von boden, wänden und türnischen lenken besucher in richtung festebene vestibule, main entrance area > floors, walls and doorframes were designed to lead visitors in direction of the festive area

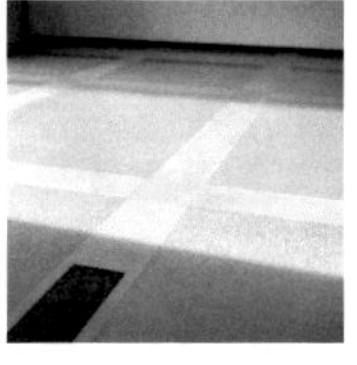
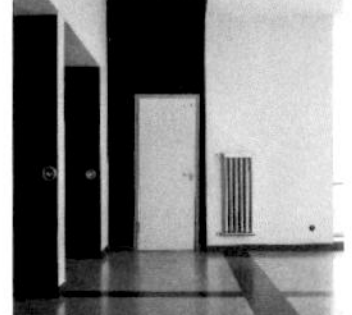

20 | 21 treppenhaus am haupteingang, treppenstufen und handlauf zum erstem stock main entrance staircase, stairs and handrail to the first floor

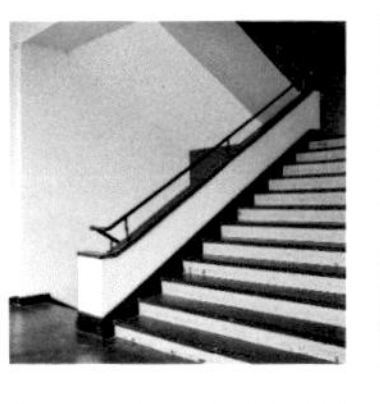
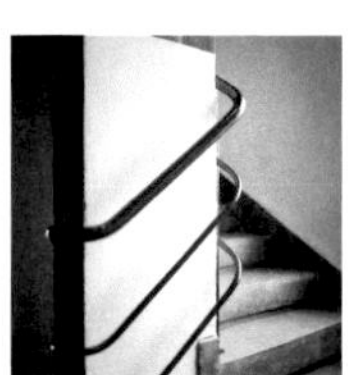

22 | 23 treppenhaus am haupteingang, treppenflucht zwischen erstem und zweitem stock | treppenabsatz zwischen erdgeschoss und erstem stock, anschnitt eines heizkörpers auf halber höhe main entrance staircase, flight of stairs between the first and second floor | landing between the ground floor and first floor, part of a radiator halfway up

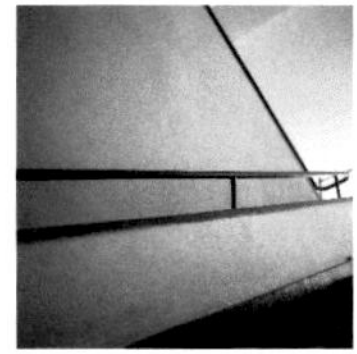
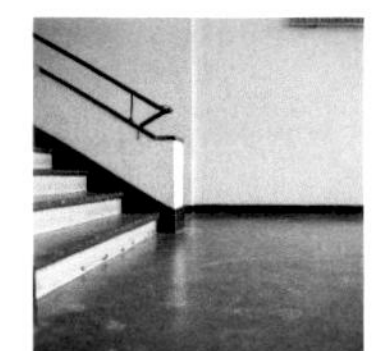

24 | 25 treppenhaus am haupteingang, brüstung und handlauf main entrance staircase, balustrade and handrail

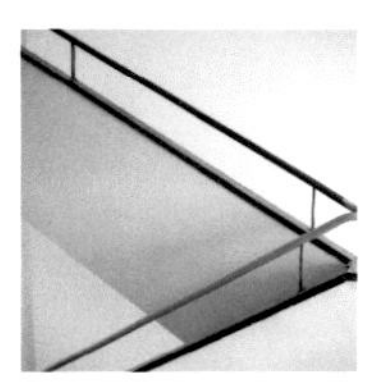
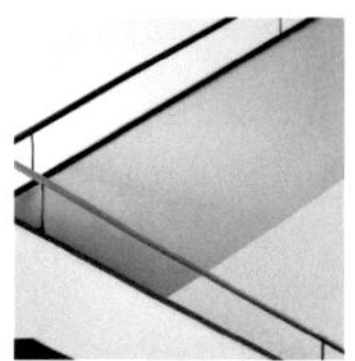

26 | 27 treppenhaus am haupteingang, treppenabsatz mit brüstung und handlauf, treppenaufgang zwischen ergeschoss und erstem stock, blick durch das fenster in richtung brücke main entrance staircase, landing with balustrade and handrail, stairs between groundfloor and first floor, view through the window in the direction of the bridge

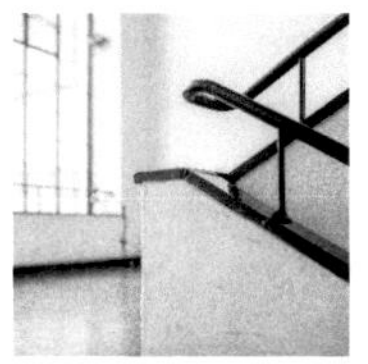
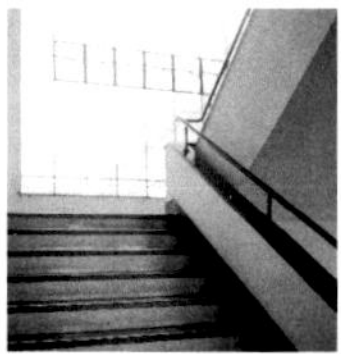

29 vestibül, erdgeschoss, blick auf die ostfassade des werkstättentrakts > der eingangsbereich diente zugleich als empfangsbereich und aussichtsplattform vestibule, ground floor, view to the east facade of the workshop wing > the entrance area served as a reception area and viewing platform

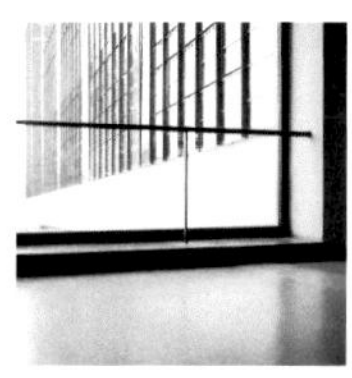

30 | 31 vestibül, zweiter stock, blick auf die ostfassade des werkstättentrakts, sessel wassily (entwurf marcel breuer) – stahlrohrkonstruktion mit schwarzer lederbespannung vestibule, second floor, view to the east facade of the workshop wing, armchair wassily (design marcel breuer) – tubular steel construction with black leather covering

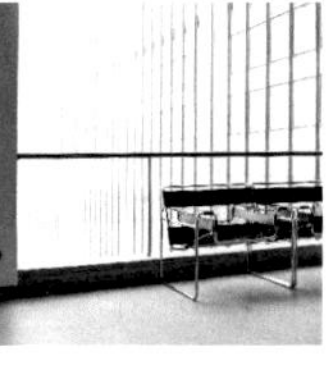

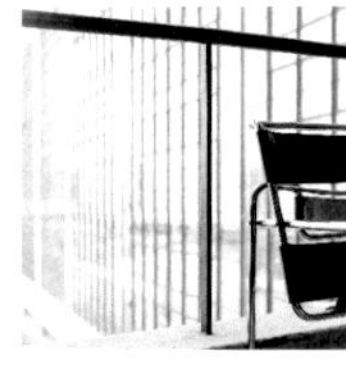

32 | 33 vestibül, zweiter stock, blick auf die ostfassade des werkstättentrakts, sessel wassily (entwurf marcel breuer) – stahlrohrkonstruktion mit schwarzer lederbespannung vestibule, second floor, view to the east facade of the workshop wing, armchair wassily (design marcel breuer) – tubular steel construction with black leather upholstery

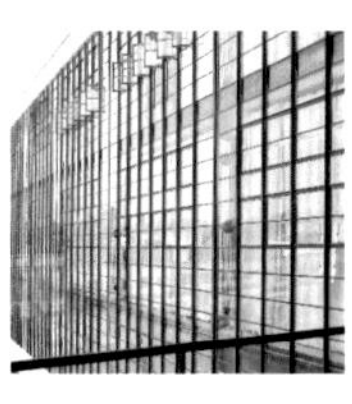

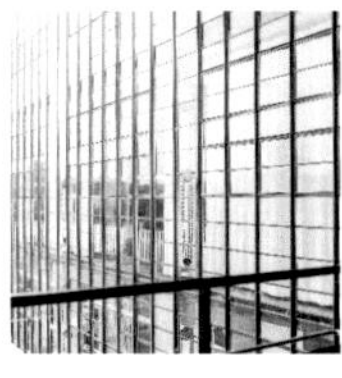

34 | 35 vestibül, erster stock, blick auf die ostfassade des werkstättentrakts > der begriff glasvorhang erscheint hier am besten nachvollziehbar – eine durchgehende fassade ohne unterbrechende stützen war neu zur zeit des baus vestibule, first floor, view to the east facade of the workshop wing > the term glass curtain seems most obvious here – a continuous facade without interrupting columns, a novelty at the time of its construction

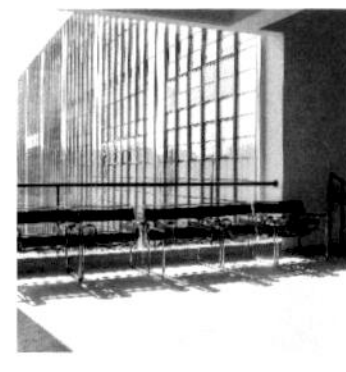

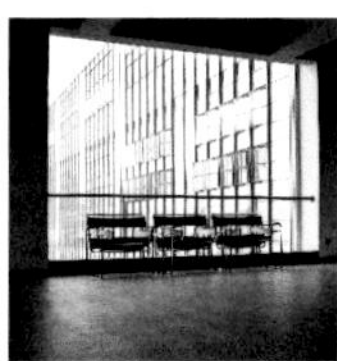

36 | 37 brücke, zweiter stock, sessel wassily (entwurf marcel breuer) stahlrohrkonstruktion mit schwarzer lederbespannung > die von marcel breuer entworfenen stahlrohrmöbel waren ideal für die industrielle produktion geeignet und eines der erfolgreichsten bauhaus-erzeugnisse bridge, second floor, armchair wassily (design marcel breuer) – tubular steel construction with black leather covering > the tubular steel furniture designed by marcel breuer were perfectly suited for industrial production and one of the most successful bauhaus products

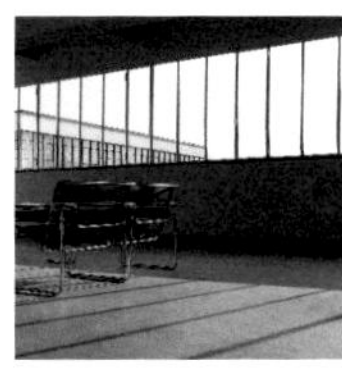

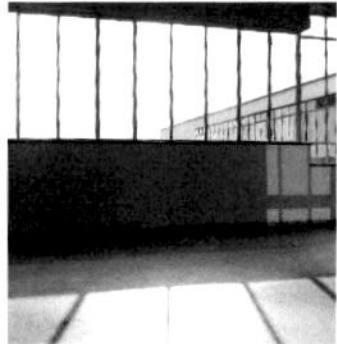

39 brücke, erster stock, neben dem gropiuszimmer, licht- und schattenspiel, lichtknopf aus bakelit bridge, first floor, next to the gropius room, play of light and shadow, light switch with push-button made of bakelite

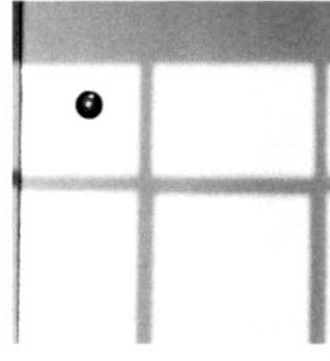

40 | 41 brücke, zweiter stock, blick in richtung werkstattflügel, licht- und schattenspiel, lichtschalter aus bakelit, pendelleuchte (entwurf marianne brandt, nachbau) bridge, second floor, view in direction of the workshop wing, play of light and shadow, light switch made of bakelite, pendant lamp (design marianne brandt, replical)

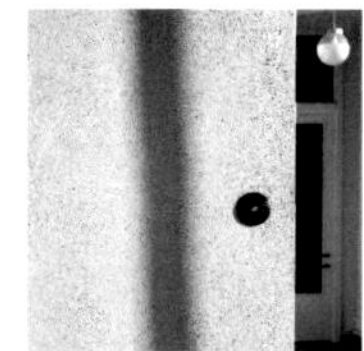
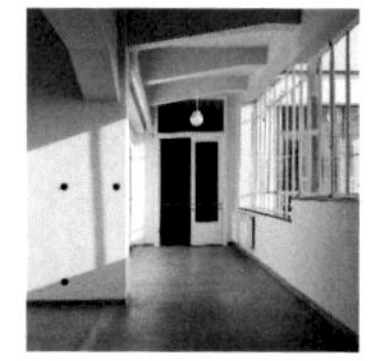

42 | 43 brücke, erster stock, blick in richtung nordflügel (technische lehranstalten) licht- und schattenspiel | perspektivische sicht bridge, first floor, view to the north wing (technische lehranstalten), play of light and shadow | perspective view

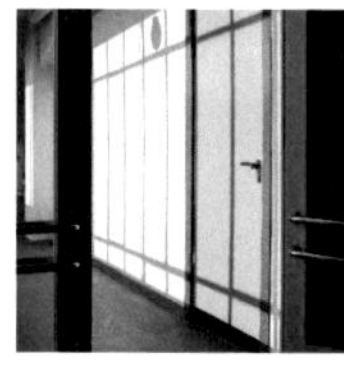
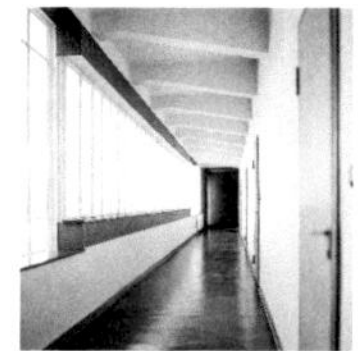

44 | 45 treppenhaus am haupteingang, treppenabsatz zwischen erstem und zweitem stock mit lichtspiel auf wand, junkers-heizkörper und pendelleuchte (entwurf marianne brandt, nachbau) main entrance stair-case, landing between the first and second floor with play of light on the wall, junkers-radiator and pendant lamp (design marianne brandt, replical)

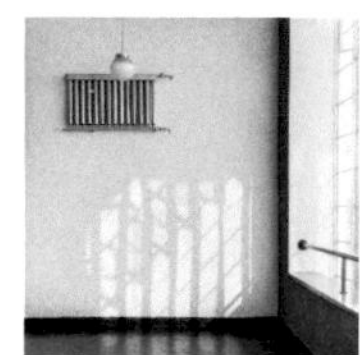
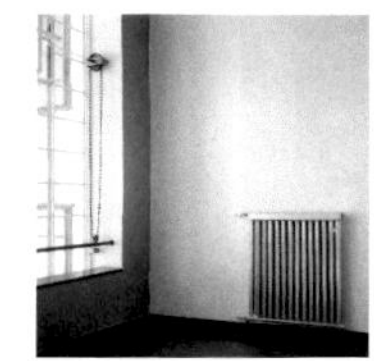

46 | 47 treppenhaus am haupteingang, treppenabsatz zum ersten stock, fensteröffnungsmechanismus aus stahl: gewindestange mit umlenkrolle und kettenzug > beispielhafte funktionalität: das aufschwenken einer reihe von fenstern wird durch leichtes ziehen eines kettenzuges erreicht main entrance staircase, landing leading to the first floor, window rotation mechanism made of steel: threaded rod with pulley and chain hoist > exemplary functionality: with a light pull on the chain a row of windows swings open

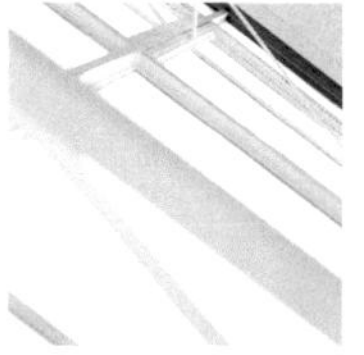
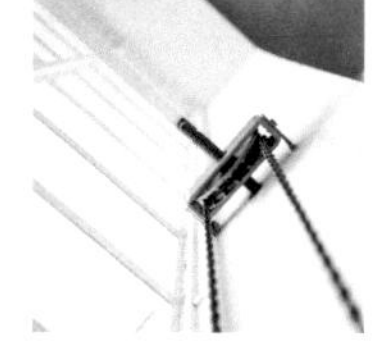

49 treppenhaus am haupteingang, treppenabsatz zum ersten stock, detail eines drehbaren fensters aus stahl main entrance staircase, landing leading to the first floor, detail of a pivotable window made of steel

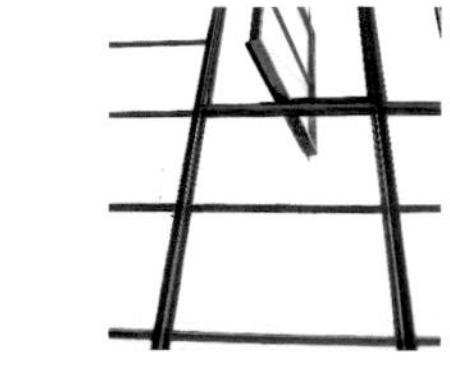

50 | 51 nordflügel (technische lehranstalten), treppenabsatz zum zweiten stock, innenansicht mit drehfenstern | werkstattflügel, blick auf die westliche glasvorhangfassade north wing (technische lehranstalten), landing leading to the second floor, interior with pivotable windows | workshop wing, view to the western glass curtain facade

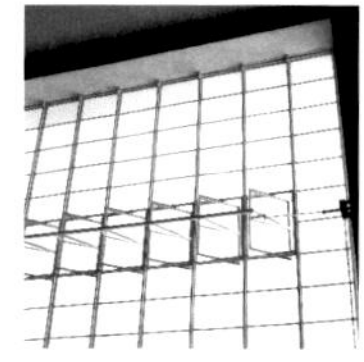
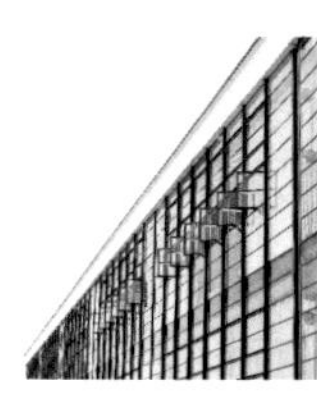

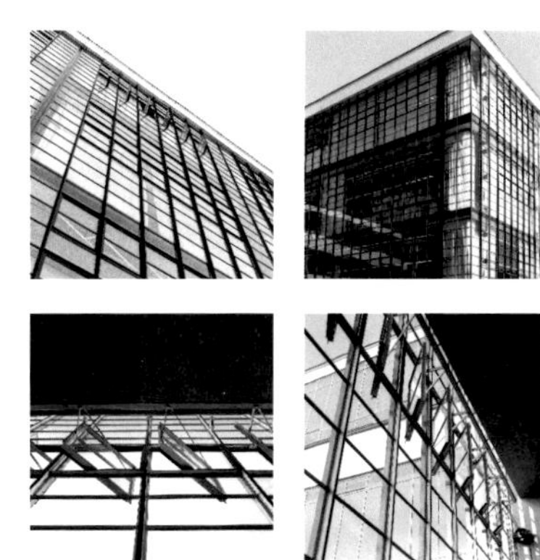

52 | 53 werkstattflügel, nördliche fassade über dem haupteingang | werkstattflügel, nordwestliche ecke workshop wing, northern facade above the main entrance | work-shop wing, north west part

54 | 55 treppenhaus am haupteingang, treppenabsatz zum ersten stock, gekuppelte drehfenster | blick auf die brücke > zum zeitpunkt des baus wurden entsprechende fenstermechanismen nur in industriellen gebäuden eingesetzt main entrance staircase, landing leading to the first floor, interconnected pivotable windows | view of the bridge > at the time of the construction similar window mechanisms were only installed in industrial buildings

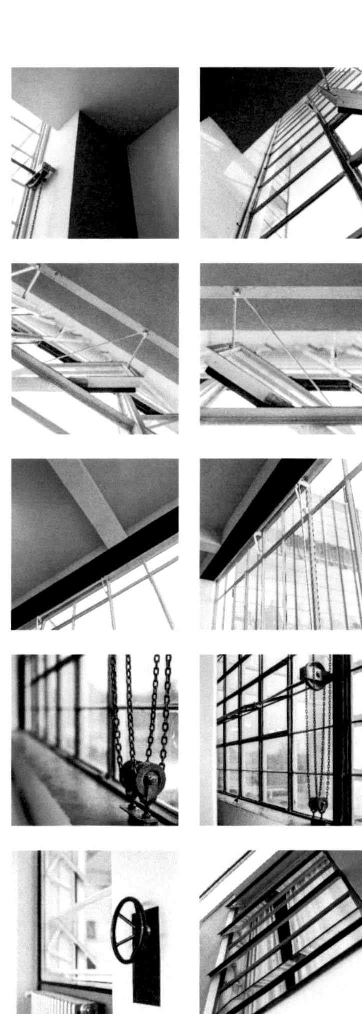

56 | 57 treppenhaus am haupteingang, treppenabsatz zum ersten stock, umlenkrolle, wand- und deckendetail | perspektivische innenansicht main entrance staircase, landing leading to the first floor, pulley, detail of the wall and ceiling | interior perspective

58 | 59 treppenhaus am haupteingang, treppenabsatz zum ersten stock, mit querstange gekuppelte drehfenster zum gleichzeitigen öffnen main entrance staircase, landing leading to the first floor, pivotable windows with a crossbar for simultaneous opening

60 | 61 brücke, erster stock, farbliche decken- und wandgestaltung, fensteröffnungsmechanismus | blick auf die nordfassade oberhalb des haupteingangs bridge, first floor, color design of ceiling and wall, window opening mechanism | view of the north facade above the main entrance

62 | 63 werkstattflügel, erdgeschoss, blick durch die östliche glasfassade (in richtung der festebene), umlenkrolle des fensteröffnungsmechanismus workshop wing, ground floor, view through the eastern glass facade (in direction of the festive area), pulley of the window opening mechanism

64 | 65 festebene, vertikal angeordnete fensterflügel mit öffnungsmechanismus, innenansicht | außenansicht festive area, vertically aligned casement windows with opening mechanism, interior | exterior

67 kantine (festebene), detail eines mensa-hockers aus gebogenem stahlrohr (entwurf marcel breuer) canteen (festive area), detail of a canteen stool made of tubular steel (design marcel breuer)

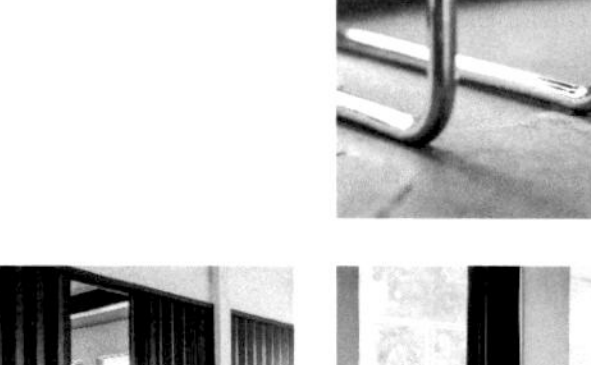

68 | 69 bühne (festebene), blick von der bauhaus-bühne richtung mensa | kantine (festebene), mensa-mobiliar (entwurf marcel breuer) und zugang zur terrasse > walter gropius hatte diesen trakt so entworfen, dass vom vestibül aus, durch die aula, über die bühne hinweg, in die mensa, mit essens-ausgabe und küche gesehen werden konnte stage (festive area), view of canteen from the bauhaus stage | canteen (festive area), canteen furniture (design marcel breuer) and access to the terrace > walter gropius constructed this section with the idea that people could see into the canteen with serving counter and kitchen from the entrance across the auditorium

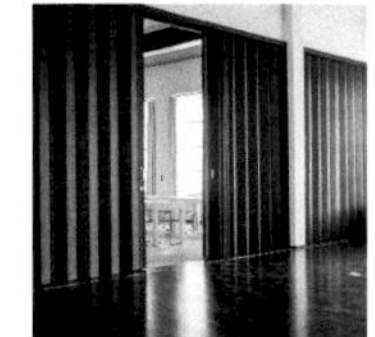

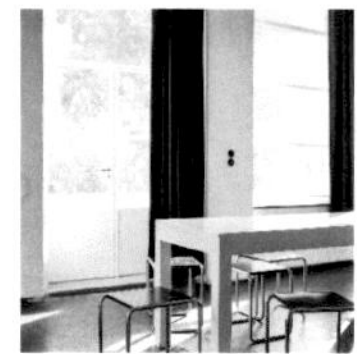

70 | 71 kantine (festebene), mensa-mobiliar (entwurf marcel breuer) und zugang zur terrasse canteen (festive area), canteen furniture (design marcel breuer) and access to the terrace

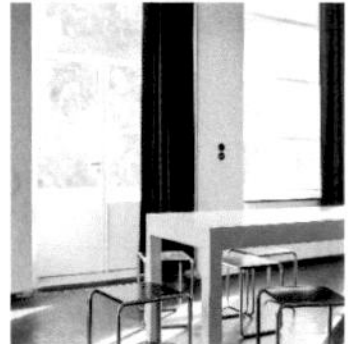

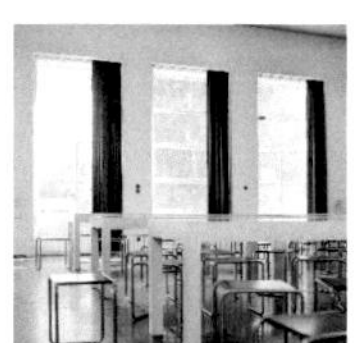

72 | 73 aula (festebene), aulagestühl (entwurf marcel breuer) – gebogenes metallrohr mit stoff-bespannung aus eisengarngewebe > das am bauhaus entwickelte eisengarngewebe wird heute noch in ähnlicher weise als zugsicherer autogurt eingesetzt auditorium (festive area), seating (design marcel breuer) – tubular steel seating with streched 'eisengarn' fabric > the fabric 'eisengarn' was developed in the bauhaus textile workshop. a similiar fabric is still used as tension safe seat belts in cars

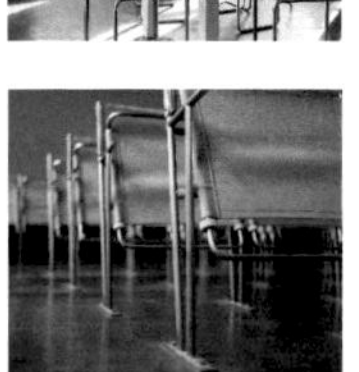

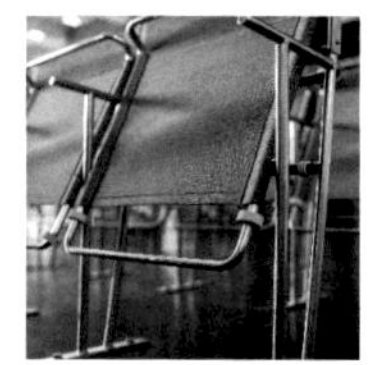

74 | 75 aula (festebene), aulagestühl (entwurf marcel breuer) – gebogenes metallrohr mit stoffbe-spannung aus eisengarngewebe auditorium (festive area), hall seating (design marcel breuer) – tubular steel seating with streched 'eisengarn' fabric

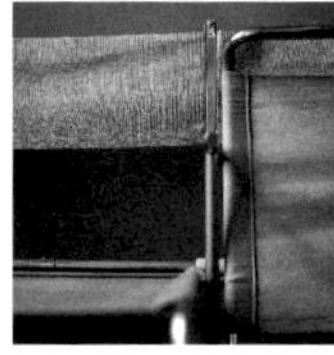

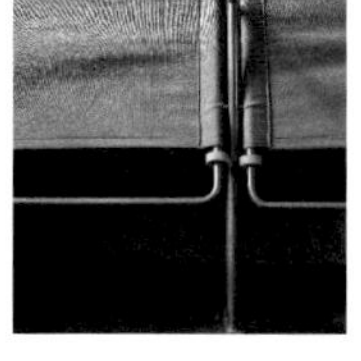

77 aula (festebene), decke mit soffitten-leuchten (entwurf max krajewski) auditorium (festive area), ceiling with tubular lighting system (design max krajewski)

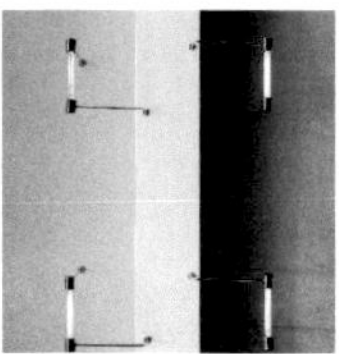

78 | 79 vestibül, decke im erdgeschoss, soffittenleuchten (entwurf max krajewski) > die führungsrohre des beleuchtungssystems wurden so ausgerichtet, dass sie besucher in richtung aula und bühne lenken vestibule, ceiling of the ground floor, tubular lighting system (design max krajewski) > the lighting system and its tubes were placed purposely to lead visitors in the direction of the auditorium and the festive area

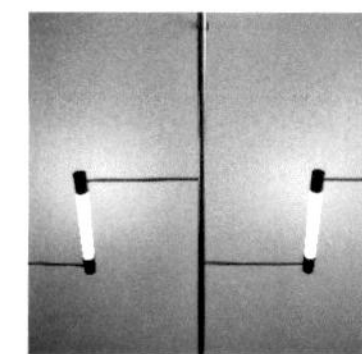
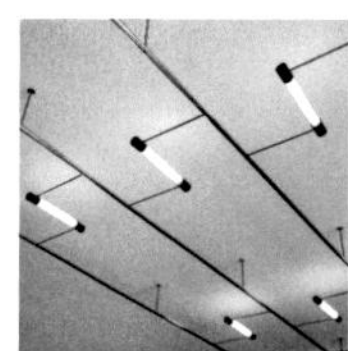

80 | 81 vestibül, decke des erdgeschosses mit soffittenleuchten (entwurf max krajewski) vestibule, ceiling of the ground floor with tubular lighting system (design max krajewski)

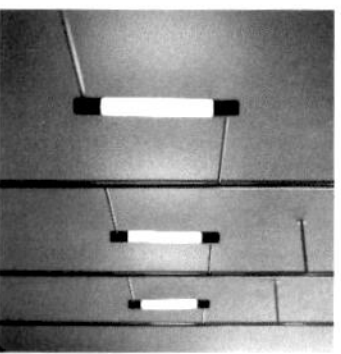
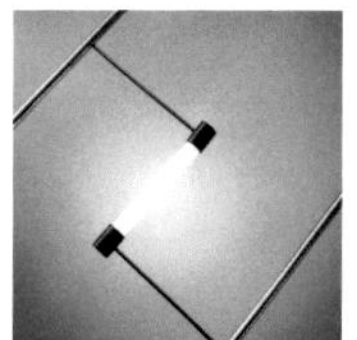

83 ateliergebäude (‚prellerhaus'), treppenhaus, detail der farbgestaltung von wand und decke (entwurf hinnerk scheper) studio building ('prellerhaus'), staircase, color design detail of the wall and ceiling (design hinnerk scheper)

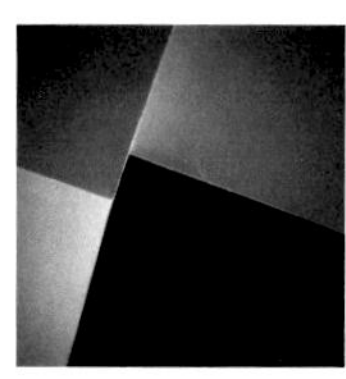

84 | 85 treppenhaus am haupteingang, treppenabsatz zum erstem stock, detail der farbgestaltung | ateliergebäude (‚prellerhaus'), treppenhaus, detail der farbgestaltung (entwurf hinnerk scheper) > farbe wurde gezielt als gestaltungsmittel zur raumbildung eingesetzt main entrance staircase, landing leading to the first floor, color design detail | studio building ('prellerhaus'), staircase, color design detail (design hinnerk scheper) > the use of color was intentional as a tool for creating space

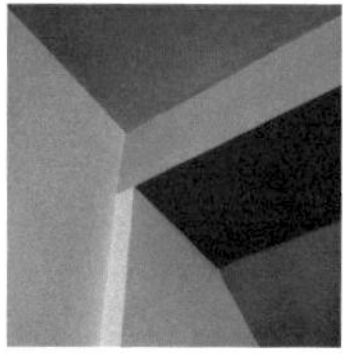
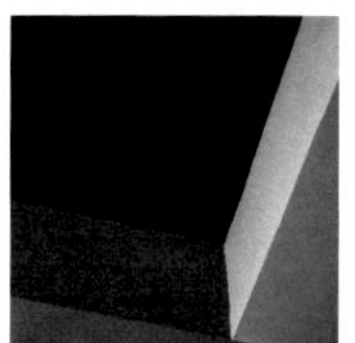

86 | 87 ateliergebäude (‚prellerhaus'), treppenhaus, detail der farbgestaltung von wand und decke (entwurf hinnerk scheper) | meisterhäuser, decke eines treppenaufgangs studio building ('prellerhaus'), staircase, color design detail of the wall and the ceiling (design hinnerk scheper) | masters' houses, staircase ceiling

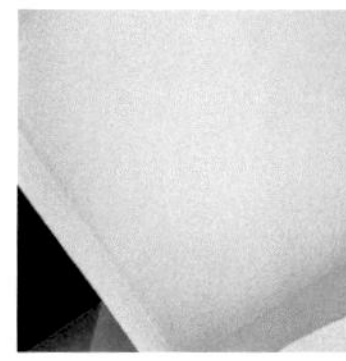
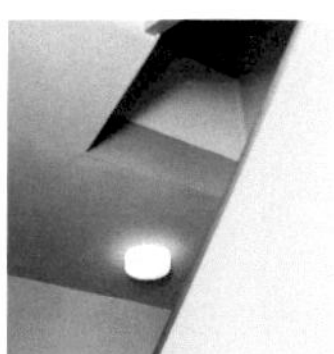

89 ateliergebäude (‚prellerhaus'), blick von der bauhausstraße auf das fensterband des treppenhauses > als verweis an die weimarer herkunft wird das gebäude auch ‚prellerhaus' genannt. der maler friedrich preller hatte studenten der kunstschule ein wohnhaus im 19. jahrhundert zur verfügung gestellt studio building ('prellerhaus'), view from the bauhausstraße of the long row of staircase windows > the studio building is also called 'prellerhaus'. the name is a reference to its origins in weimar. the painter friedrich preller opened his home for the weimar art school students in the 19th century

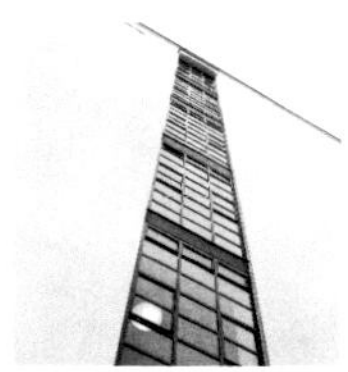

90 | 91 ateliergebäude (‚prellerhaus'), blick von der bauhausstraße auf das fensterband des treppenhauses studio building ('prellerhaus'), view from the bauhausstraße to the long row of staircase windows

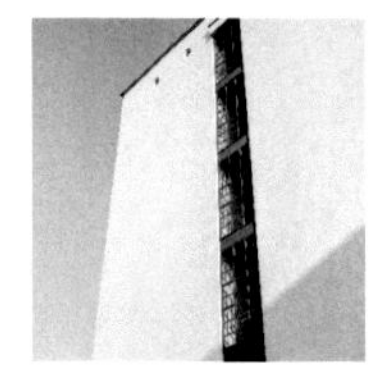
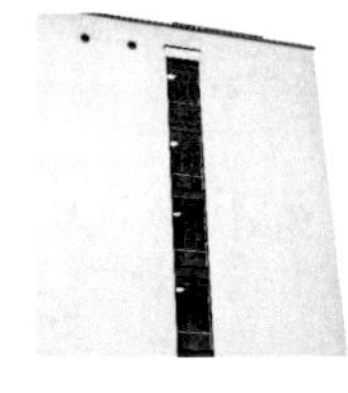

92 | 93 blick auf festebene und werkstattflügel, südost-ansicht | ateliergebäude (‚prellerhaus'), blick von der bauhausstraße auf die erste balkonreihe > das ‚prellerhaus' war das erste in eine hochschule integrierte studentenwohnheim in deutschland view of the festive area and the workshop wing, southeast view | studio building ('prellerhaus'), view from the bauhausstraße to the first row of balconies > the 'prellerhaus' was the first student residence integrated into a college in germany

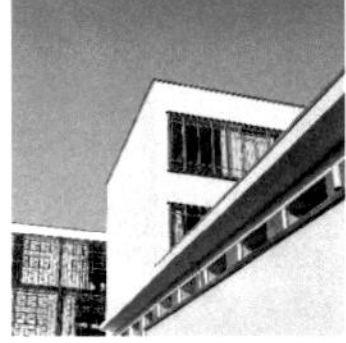
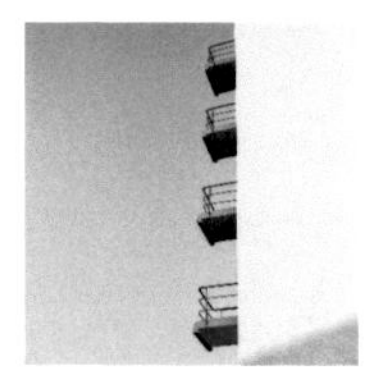

94 | 95 ateliergebäude (‚prellerhaus'), südliche fassade, blick auf umlaufende balkone > aus meiner sicht könnten manche bauten in tel aviv hier ihren ursprung haben studio building ('prellerhaus'), south facade, view of the circumferential balconies > in my opinion some buildings in tel aviv could have their origins here

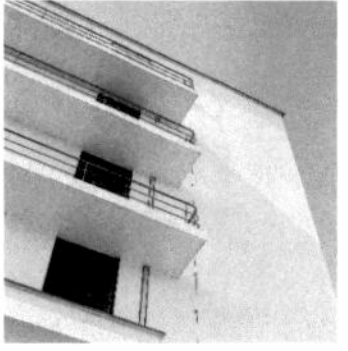
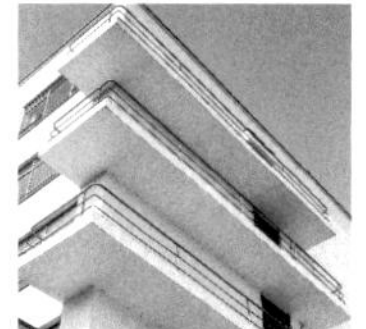

96 | 97 ateliergebäude (‚prellerhaus'), südliche fassade, blick auf umlaufende balkone studio building ('prellerhaus'), south facade, view onto the circumferential balconies

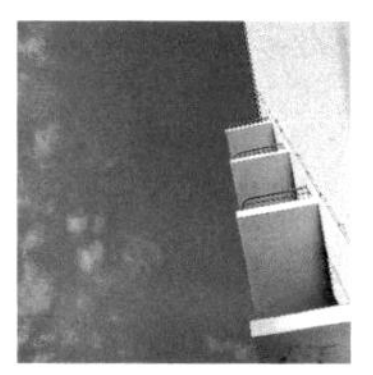
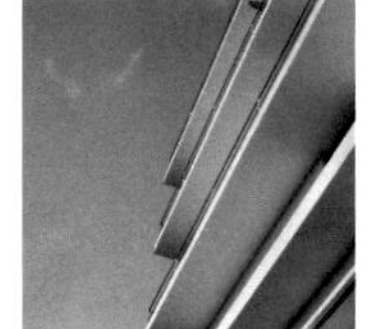

98 werkstattflügel, bauhaus schriftzug an der südseite (in anlehnung an einen schriftentwurf von herbert bayer) workshop wing, bauhaus lettering on the south side (following a type design by herbert bayer)

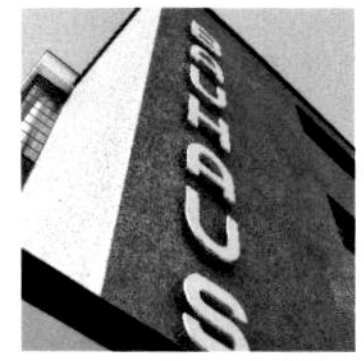

101 gaststätte ‚kornhaus' an der elbe, detail des verglasten umgangs, konstruktion aus glas und metall (entwurf carl fieger) restaurant 'kornhaus' next to the river elbe, detail of the glazed passage, glass and metal construction (design carl fieger)

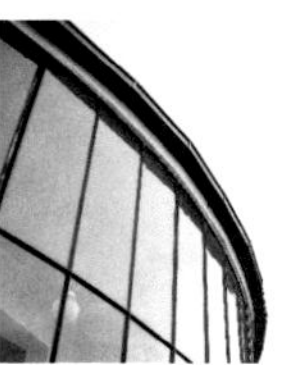

102 | 103 gaststätte ‚kornhaus' an der elbe (entwurf carl fieger), detail des verglasten umgangs, konstruktion aus glas und metall, pendelleuchte (entwurf marianne brandt, nachbau) | blick von der elbuferseite des deiches, im vordergrund der verglaste umgang

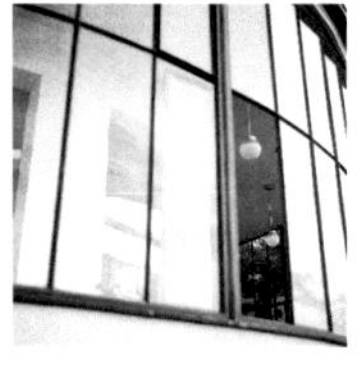
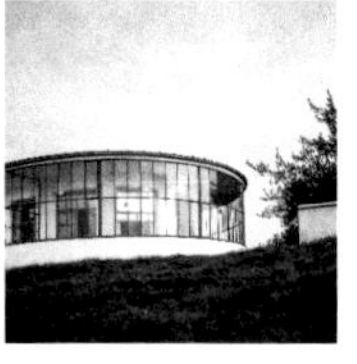

102 | 103 restaurant 'kornhaus' next to the river elbe (design carl fieger), detail of the glazed passage, glass and metal construction, pendant lamp (design marianne brandt, replical) | view from the riverside onto the embankment, in the foreground the glazed passage

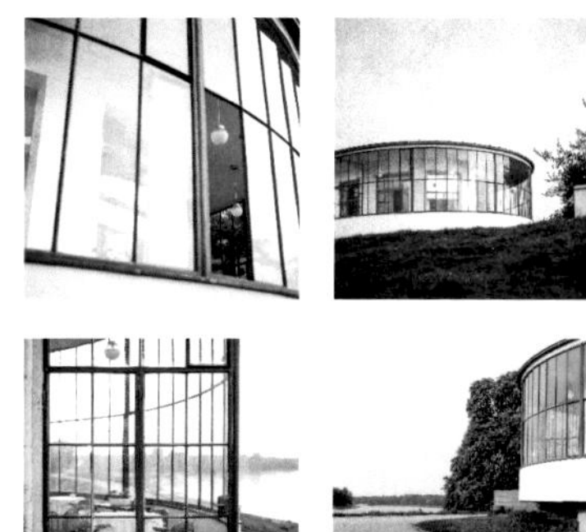

104 | 105 gaststätte ‚kornhaus' an der elbe (entwurf carl fieger), blick auf den zugang und die einrichtung im verglasten umgang | blick von der kornhausstraße auf sockel und detail des verglasten umgangs restaurant 'kornhaus' next to the river elbe (design carl fieger), view to the entrance of the glazed passage and its furniture | view from the kornhaus-straße detail of the glazed passage, glass and metal construction

106 deichkrone am ‚kornhaus', blick auf die romantische elbe in richtung norden dike top at 'kornhaus', picturesque view to the north of the elbe

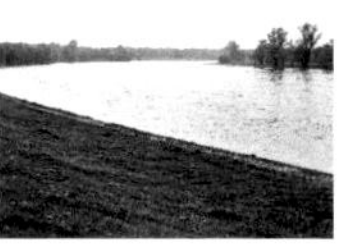

122 gaststätte ‚kornhaus' an der elbe (entwurf carl fieger), innenbereich mit gästen restaurant 'kornhaus' (design carl fieger), interior with guests

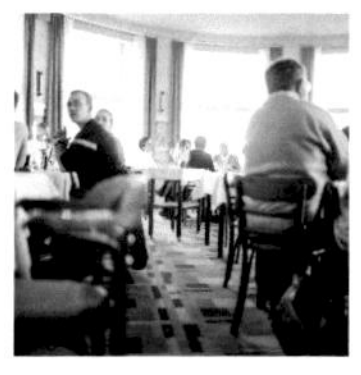

127 brücke, ‚gropiusdrücker' (entwurf walter gropius und adolf meyer) zum direktorenzimmer bridge, 'gropius door handle' (design walter gropius and adolf meyer) leading to the director's office

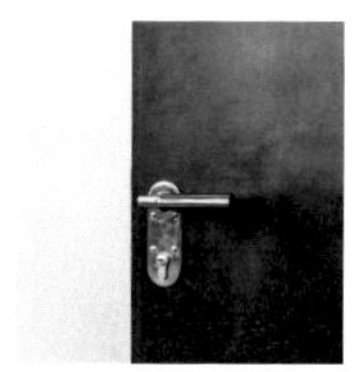

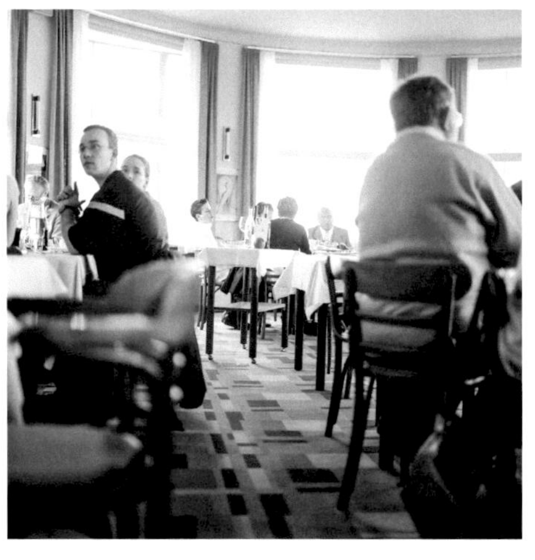

danke! thank you!

mein dank geht an alle, die dieses buch ermöglicht haben: harald theiss für seinen unermüdlichen einsatz, ohne ihn würde es dieses buch nicht geben. wiebke loeper für text und unterstützung. walter scheiffele, peter thieme, betina müller, torsten köchlin und gerald christ für fachliche beratung und kulinarische ablenkung. carmen billows und oliver shaw für sprachliche hilfe. uta grosenick, silvia koch und rebecca wilton von distanz für ihre geduld und max color für den feinschliff. den ‚förderinnen' vom auswärtigen amt, sowie allen ‚bauhaus'-mitarbeiterinnen für ihre wohlwollende unterstützung, im speziellen margot rumler vom bildarchiv der stiftung bauhaus dessau. mein besonderer dank gilt peter koehl, der mir die grundlagenlehre des bauhauses nahegebracht hat, und bodo müller, durch den ich raum und fläche richtig zu sehen gelernt habe. und ein ganz herzliches dankeschön an meine frau ina für ihre ermutigung und kreative unterstützung, sowie an meine eltern, ohne die ich nicht wäre, was ich bin. special thanks to all who helped me make this book possible: harald theiss for his endless dedication, without him this book would not exist. wiebke loeper for her text and kind support. walter scheiffele, peter thieme, betina müller, torsten köchlin and gerald christ for their advice and culinary distraction. carmen billows and oliver shaw for their linguistic support. uta grosenick, silvia koch and rebecca wilton from distanz for their patience and max color for the fine-tuning. the 'supporters' from the federal foreign office, as well as all the 'bauhaus' staff for their kind support, especially margot rumler from the image archive of the bauhaus foundation dessau. my very special thanks go to peter koehl, who made me familiar with the bauhaus basic course and to bodo müller through whom i started to see space and surface in a relevant way. last but not least a loving thank you to my wife for all her encouragement and creative support and to my parents who made me become what i am.

zur person about

STEFAN BERG

stefan berg ist fotograf. er setzt sich vorwiegend mit den themen arbeit, identität und bildung auseinander. er wurde 1971 in bielefeld geboren und hat in heidelberg fotograf für industrie und werbung gelernt. während längerer aufenthalte in belgien und frankreich arbeitete er für agenturen, zeitschriften und regierungseinrichtungen. nach seiner qualifizierung zum fotografenmeister war er als ausbilder, studioleiter und dozent tätig. darauf aufbauend studierte er komunikationsdesign zum diplom an der fachhochschule potsdam.
fotografische arbeiten von stefan berg waren in deutschland, frankreich und belgien zu sehen. eine serie wurde in die sammlung der deutschen botschaft paris, eine andere in die des goethe-instituts brüssel aufgenommen. als lehrbeauftragter für fotografie war er unter anderem an der udk berlin, dem lette-verein berlin, der fh potsdam und der hochschule anhalt in dessau tätig. stefan berg lebt und arbeitet in berlin. stefan berg is a photographer. he deals mainly with the subjects of work, identity and education. he learned his craft as industry and advertising photographer in heidelberg. during longer stays in belgium and france he worked for agencies, magazines and government institutions. after his training to a master level in photography he worked as instructor, studio manager and lecturer. he then acquired a diploma in communication design at the university of applied sciences in potsdam.
photographic works from stefan berg have been shown in germany, france and belgium. stefan berg's work is included in the collection of the german embassy in paris and the collection of the goethe-institute in brussels.
stefan berg was a universtity lecturer at the berlin university of the arts, the lette-verein berlin, the university of applied sciences in potsdam and the anhalt university of applied sciences in dessau. stefan berg lives and works in berlin.

bergwerke.net

HARALD THEISS

harald theiss ist kunsthistoriker, kurator und autor. er organisiert u. a. ausstellungen zu gesellschaftsrelevanten themen, betreut private kunstsammlungen und kunst im stadtraum und am bau projekte. harald theiss lebt und arbeitet in berlin harald theiss is art historian, curator and writer. he organizes i.a. exhibitions on socially relevant issues and takes care of private art collections and art in architecture and public space projects. harald theiss lives and works in berlin

haraldtheiss.de

WIEBKE LOEPER

wiebke loeper ist fotografin, künstlerin und seit 2008 professorin für fotografie an der fh potsdam am fachbereich design. ihre arbeiten loten den zusammenhang biografischer erfahrung und gesellschaftlicher transformationsprozesse aus wiebke loeper is a photographer and artist and since 2008 professor of photography at the university of applied sciences in the department of design in potsdam. her works pinpoint the relationship of biographical experiences and social transformation processes

wiebkeloeper.de

impressum imprint

herausgeber editor harald theiss

idee und fotografie idea and photography stefan berg

konzept und zusammenstellung concept and composition harald theiss

gestaltung design stefan berg
beratung mentoring wiebke loeper

texte texts wiebke loeper, harald theiss
übersetzung translation benjamin t. busch
s. pp. 8–9; s. pp. 110–111
lektorat copy editing DISTANZ verlag, berlin

lithografie image editing max color, berlin

produktion production management DISTANZ verlag

gesamtherstellung printing and binding
DZA druckerei zu altenburg gmbh

vertrieb distribution
edel germany gmbh
www.edel.com
distanz@edel.com

ISBN 978-3-95476-231-6
printed in germany

erschienen im published by
DISTANZ verlag
www.distanz.de

mit freundlicher unterstützung von with kind support of thonet gmbh, frankenberg

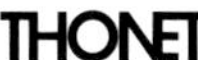

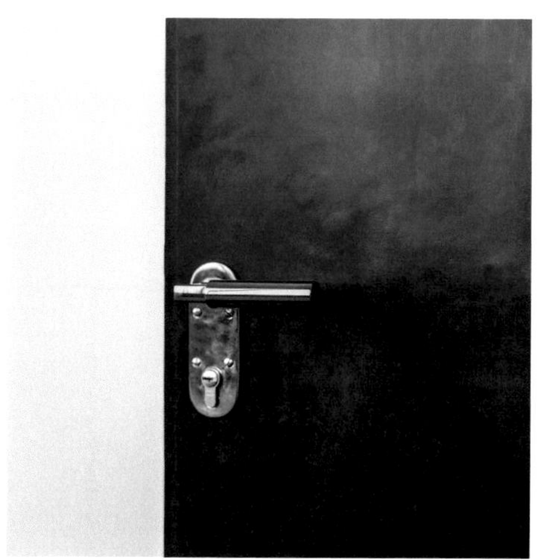